Conquering Your
Quarter-Life Crisis

CONQUERING YOUR *Quarter-Life* CRISIS

HOW TO GET YOUR SHIT TOGETHER IN YOUR 20s

KALI ROGERS

THOUGHT
CATALOG
Books

Copyright © 2016 by The Thought & Expression Co.

All rights reserved. Designed by KJ Parish. Cover photography by © Jason Flynn

Published by Thought Catalog Books, a division of The Thought & Expression Co., Williamsburg, Brooklyn. Founded in 2010, Thought Catalog is a website and imprint dedicated to your ideas and stories. We publish fiction and non-fiction from emerging and established writers across all genres. For general information and submissions: manuscripts@thoughtcatalog.com.

First edition, 2017

ISBN: 978-1945796357

Printed and bound in the United States.

10 9 8 7 6 5 4 3 2 1

I rent a room and I fill the spaces with
Wood in places to make it feel like home
But all I feel's alone.
It might be a quarter-life crisis
Or just the stirring in my soul.
Either way I wonder sometimes
About the outcome.
Of a still verdictless life.
Am I living it right?

—John Mayer

Rock bottom became the solid foundation on which I rebuilt my life.

—J.K. Rowling

CONTENTS

Part 1

The Quarter-Life Crisis

1

Fuck the Quarter-Life Crisis

Yep. Just fuck it.

Let me guess: at this point, you are either so sad you can't stop crying (make sure to not drip all over this book, hopefully it has something valuable in it), so angry that you're seeing a deep shade of red, or so exhausted that someone bought you this book and you are forcing yourself to read it so you can at least feel like you're making an effort to stop this horrific cycle of growing up.

I'm with you.

I define the quarter-life crisis as that anxiety-provoking period of time between building towards entering into adulthood and actually entering into real, full-out adulthood. It's like the grown-up version of puberty, but instead of morphing into awkward, hungry humans, we grow into tired and confused humans.

Within the span of a few months, all of your life decisions AND mistakes fall entirely on your shoulders. The load on your shoulders just increased tenfold. And instead of having an easy guideline to follow in order to ensure success, we have to wing it.

3

Unfortunately, this phase of anxiety, self-doubt, hopelessness and confusion can last for months, or in my case, years. And P.S.—suffering from the quarter-life crisis has nothing to do with maturity, intelligence, or preparedness. It doesn't mean you're a failure, it doesn't mean you're pathetic, and it doesn't mean you have bad luck. The quarter-life crisis can attack anyone between the ages of 18 and 30. And it is no joke.

In fact, the quarter-life crisis is a soul-sucking, nail-biting, hair-pulling, anxiety-provoking black hole that can absolutely consume you if you're not careful.

It's quite poetic, really. Instead of having the time of your life at your prime, you feel like your life is over before it even started.

So I want to tell you that this phase is normal. I know older generations love to glamorize their 20 something years just a tad so you are going to have to ignore them for a bit. Because unlike Hollywood portrays, this decade is full of learning lessons, royally screwing up, and starting over from scratch. I would say year 20 through 29 of your life is basically going to consist of you throwing a bunch of shit on a wall and seeing what actually sticks. And then having to clean up what doesn't.

There is absolutely nothing glamorous about it.

But you don't have to be alone in this. You don't have to keep telling yourself that you're a freak for not feeling like your most fabulous, peak self at age 25. Because the reality is your astute self-awareness and high expectations are probably exacerbating this quarter-life crisis, but they are also going to pull you out of it.

Hopefully this book will serve as a guide for you. I cover self-exploration, adult friendships, career options, relationship woes, and mental tricks to snap you out of this funk. Be patient with yourself. Take everything in with a solid amount of deep breathing and remind yourself that you are going to push through.

2

My Quarter-Life Crisis

Let's talk about how I'm qualified to school you on getting out of your quarter-life crisis.

I bet you think my life is just PERFECT. I mean here I am, sitting here in my University of Texas flannel jammies writing a book chock-full of lessons on how you can turn your life around. So I must really have my shit together.

That's not *entirely* true. I'll be completely honest with you: I spent a solid three years in my quarter-life crisis.

Yep. It lasted from age 21 to age 24. So as much as you're hurting right now, I promise you, I've been there. And I was trapped there for three years, and let's just say I made myself nice and cozy.

Ugh. It was awful. Just awful.

I seriously believe the worst year of my life was when I was 22 years old. 22! The year after you are legally allowed to drink! The year you are finally supposed to be independent! The year you still have an amazing metabolism and are immune to hangovers and have an arsenal of optimism and you can actually go to a grown-up happy hour with your grownup friends and talk about grown-up stuff! That is not what 22 looked like for me.

It's funny, too, because 22 is my lucky number. Let me tell you, this universe has a really fucked up sense of humor.

So let's figure out how my 22-year-old self hated life so much.

I'd like to blame it on my parent's divorce. That would be so much easier. After 20+ years of marriage, my parents decided to call it quits not too long after I left the house for college. Someone had an affair, someone was pretty upset about it, and both parties decided it was better to move on with their lives. It wasn't a fun time to be a part of the Rogers clan. My parents, like any other parents, weren't actually sure how to handle a divorce themselves let alone how to handle it with adult kids. We weren't young enough to require a full-blown plan of attack for damage control, but we weren't old enough to totally understand that our parents were just people, either.

Isn't that a crazy phenomenon? Learning that your parents are just human beings like yourself? Realizing that they don't know what they're doing any more than you do—they just had to figure it out because age kept pushing them forward? It's a super frightening realization. It really pushed me into a different kind of adulthood than I had imagined.

But if I have to be honest, dealing with divorced parents wasn't that difficult; especially when I finally let one of them out of the doghouse. Instead of having one phone call, I had two. Instead of seeing both my parents at Christmas, I went to one house and then another. Instead of seeing them as a unit, I saw them as two utterly confused, but amazing individuals. There was a newfound effort in becoming close with my parents I hadn't had to exercise before. It might actually be one of the better things in my life to happen to me—but then again, that's my annoyingly persistent silver-lining perspective shining through.

I was around 20 years old when all of this really came to a head. My dad had officially moved out, my mom had officially started her healing process, and the family started navigating what four separate individuals with one common last name looked like.

I was fine, really. Until I met John.

I was heading into my final stretch of my junior year of college when I decided to finally end things with my long distance athletic, smart, hunky, totally clueless boyfriend, Lucas. Honestly, my relationship with Lucas had turned into a massive disappointment just hanging on for dear life. It was comfortable and consistent and annoying like that scratchy old sweater you pull out every Christmas to wear for family dinner and promise yourself "never again."

I traced back the start of our inevitable doom to the day I called Lucas to tell him my parents were getting divorced. Like a good reliable boyfriend, he promised to get on the next flight to come console me.

Instead, he called me the next morning and pretended like the conversation had never happened. And I stayed with him a full year more because...?

Thank God for the *Twilight* series that educated me on what REAL love should look like. Yes, I'm kidding. But also yes, I did read that entire series over Christmas break instead of hanging with Lucas so maybe I wasn't such a stellar girlfriend, either.

Anywho, we finally broke up. He wasn't a bad guy, and I actually felt really guilty about it. But I was ready to party. I was ready to make out. I was ready to feel like a damn debutante, being newly ushered into the world of entitled douchebags who couldn't WAIT to talk about their rich daddy's business back home.

It took me about two solid make outs before I dumped my party girl persona and went right back to being the boring, yet very loyal, plus one.

How boring, guys. I didn't even last two weeks! Instead, I did what any obnoxious serial monogamist does and fell for the first guy who was nice to me.

Our first date? Trulucks. Our first kiss? Don't really remember. Our first REAL sexual experience? In a LAKE. A damn romantic LAKE y'all. It doesn't get much better than that.

He introduced me as his girlfriend before we had even defined the relationship, which is basically the same thing as a proposal this day in age. He talked about starting a life together post college and how I was "out of his league." We held hands in public, he took me home to meet his (amazing) family, we stayed up late at night singing and playing guitar and talking about how all of our dreams were going to come true together. We watched *Gossip Girl* together for Chrissake.

I was in love for the first time in my life, and I wasn't going to let anyone take it away from me.

That summer was arguably the best summer of my life. I was in a haze. Pretty sure I bombed the LSAT because I spent the majority of my time re-reading our text messages and stalking him on Facebook.

As fall approached, I noticed a slight shift but didn't seem to care too much. He wasn't hanging out with me as much, but, you know, school and stuff. I couldn't take it too seriously; after all, we were in love. Right?

Halloween was approaching and we had gone together to

pick out our Halloween costumes. I was Hannah Montana—yikes—and because he refused to play along, I told him to wear jeans and a vest and go as Nick Jonas. Pop stars! SO adorbs! (I am actually cringing writing this.) I was so excited to attend our final Halloween party of college—not only because we were seniors and could actually drink at this event legally—but also because my baby brother was a freshman in college and had been asked to attend the party as date! YAY!!! What on earth could go wrong???

Wellllllp I forgot my ID—not once, but twice—(that was a fun car ride back and forth), picked a fight with John because he wanted to smoke cigarettes with brat face McGee—the same girl who's response to my gushing "John told me he loved me!" was "why does he lie to people?"—and ended up walking home by myself.

Author's note: I promise you I have grown up by now. And if it's any consolation last Halloween I was the skeleton from David S. Pumpkins and the year before that I was Piper from *Orange is the New Black* and looked super awful in a funny but sad kind of way.

The next morning, I received the black licorice of all text messages. "We need to talk." Ah, shit. I crawled into his white Tahoe passenger seat and he proceeded to drive one city block before dumping me straight on my bum.

Kali: *"But you said we were going to get married!"*
John: *"I know. I'm sorry."*
Kali: *"How could you do this?"*
John: *"This just isn't going to work out."*

Kali: *"Pull the car over, I can't breathe."*
John: *"OK."*

Pulls car over, waits approximately 5 seconds for me to de-board, and screeches away.

I remember calling my mom, barely able to breathe. I managed to squeak out that John had dumped me, and that I was standing in front of my sorority house (I am aware that I am a cliché), too scared and embarrassed to walk inside because hardly any of my friends had ever seen me cry.

That's right. After I ended a 2+ year relationship?—no visible tears. When I totally forgot to fill in the scantron on my Chemistry test, inevitably failing?—no visible tears. My parents got a fucking DIVORCE?—no visible tears.

I'm sure I probably cried over those three instances in the privacy of the communal showers—especially the Chemistry test, how on earth did I manage that?—but I had no witnesses. So as far as everyone else was concerned, I was the Ice Queen. I had a cold-button heart and no one was going to break me. Until my mommy made me go inside.

I cried for weeks. I lost weight and then gained it all back plus ten pounds (WHAT A TIME TO BE ALIVE). My friends saw me snot-nosed and puffy-eyed so many times that I think they forgot I had relatively normal coloration in my face. My bestie Caroline rubbed my back while I dry heaved every other night for a month. Poor thing. There is nothing I wouldn't do for that girl from here on out—I'm pretty sure half her T-shirts are drenched in Kali boogers. It took months before reality emerged from the wreckage.

John wasn't the perfect boyfriend. In fact, he was a shitty boyfriend. And he got so fed up with me letting him be so shitty that he got bored with me.

Case in point:

- When we went to a friend's lake house and I got the stomach flu, he sent me home with a buddy of his who was going home early so he could stay and party another night. I threw up for two days straight.
- For my 21st birthday, he came in town with a friend and went to dinner with me. Yes, he brought a friend I barely knew. Not a huge deal…but then he refused to go out or buy me a birthday drink for a celebration.
- He talked shit about me to his friends on G-chat. For real. Like who talks shit about their girlfriend in writing AND leaves it open on their computer? Idiot.
- He never once agreed to hang out with my friends even though I invited him on numerous occasions. And who wouldn't want to hang out with Caroline? Freak.
- He would consistently go to his female friend's box seats for football games and not invite me, nor ask the host to invite me. Ever. Apparently, I was an embarrassment. Or more likely, I wasn't cool enough to hang.
- He always wanted me to smoke pot. Which I realized later meant that he wanted me to shut the hell up and chill out. But you know what John I have a lot of my mind so no I don't want your silencing drugs, okkkkk?
- My family's finances were an intriguing topic during our relationship. He was very interested in if I had a

trust fund (lol k) and sized me up next to his female friends' generational wealth. Proudly, I did not measure up.

- He continuously told me I was too good for him. Which, as a note, when someone says that, please believe them.

Good lord. How did I take this person seriously? How did I let my confidence get so low that I would allow someone to dick me around for months and then get the satisfaction of dumping me?

Honestly, things didn't get much better. I became so consumed with proving to everyone that I was better than being dumped by some asshole who called me clingy, that pretty much everything I did for a solid six months was meant to manipulate others' perceptions of me.

After my days of following the trail John left around campus were gone (he essentially had a blonde shadow for three months) I decided to get my life together by applying for anything and everything I thought would impress my peers.

I applied for Teach for America without the slightest passion for teaching. Thank God the admissions team knew their shit and did not accept me. Poor kids wouldn't have stood a chance with me at the helm. I got my LSAT score back. Turns out being a lawyer wasn't really in the cards, either. And another dodged bullet by society, might I add. I also decided to date every douchebag on campus for approximately three days just to make sure everyone knew I "still had it." Going on a campus crusade to prove I was still kissable probably only convinced others the only thing I actually had was HPV. (I actually don't, I swear!)

So yeah, my "look at me, I'm adulting!" plans for post-grad crashed like Jenga tower at the hands of a five-year-old.

I resorted to my backup plan: counseling.

Because there is NOTHING better for the field of counseling than a shit show 22 year old looking to gather up the ashes of her former functioning life.

In my defense, I had always been good at talking to others. Caroline always said there would be a line outside of my dorm room because girls would want my advice on something. I always found that hilarious because it's not like my life was perfectly together, but I did a good job slipping into the five-inch pumps or ugly ass camp Tevas that someone else was wearing. (Get it? I could walk a mile in someone else's shoes. Ha.) I genuinely enjoyed listening to stories and giving feedback. And it turns out, I was usually right.

Trust me, it was shocking to me as well.

My only beef with counseling is that it wasn't sexy enough. Whenever I told people I was interested in the profession, they would say "Oh my gawd, you have to sit there and listen to people's problems all day? Gross. No thank you. Have you looked into law?"

Funny you mention that, Karen. I have looked into law. Thanks for the reminder. Have a blessed day.

Nobody gasped and said, "Wow, congratulations, you're so smart!" Nobody really cared at all. It wasn't inspiring or interesting or different. It was more par for the course. Yep, Kali—the girl who likes to talk about feelings and shit wants to go be a counselor. It was such a let down because all I wanted was to prove to everyone else that I was worth something. That was my life's mission. And I felt like I was failing.

I got to Dallas to attend graduate school and was bound and

determined to find a job. For starters, I was living at home, so that wasn't much of an ego boost. I was there for my mom, which was nice. She probably (hopefully) liked the company. But with my attitude I might have dragged her down. Sorry, mom!

Grad school was inherently part time, and let's be real—SMU admissions only required a 3.0 to waive the GRE, so I wasn't anticipating a challenging course load. The only reason I even went to this school is because I had spent 9 grueling months studying for the WRONG entrance exam. Most counseling schools weren't impressed with my mediocre LSAT score so it was off to SMU we go!

I applied for about 200 jobs, give or take, to fill the gaps. I heard back from one, about 3 months ago. Considering this was 2010 and it is now 2016, I think it's safe to say my conversion rate for job applications to interviews was 0%.

Instead of landing some glamorous job at *D Magazine* (#dream) or hell, even daycare nanny at a local preschool, I got a job waiting tables on the sage advice of my professor. Three months later, I was promoted to bartender (my first promotion!) and things were somewhat on the up and up!

Something had clicked within the past few months. Maybe it was being away from my college crew and getting back to my roots. Maybe it was having the rude awakening that life wasn't supposed to unfold the way I wanted it to. Maybe (definitely) it was the counseling program rubbing off on me and I was becoming more self-aware. But whatever it was, I was letting go of others' perceptions of me and zeroed in on what I wanted. I was leaving the past behind, and slowly coming into my own again.

And then I was sexually assaulted by Lucas's best friend, Ben.

Who was coincidentally my best friend, too. I mean, are you fucking kidding me?

Had I been drinking that night? You bet your ass. It was Saturday night, I was out with friends for like the fifth time in four months, and I was ready to start enjoying my 20s. I was finally bouncing back from feeling like a complete loser, so toasting to a round of vodka sodas seemed appropriate. In fact, being able to hang out with Ben was a relief.

Now, Ben wasn't the guy you would set your sister up with on a date. Everyone knew deep down he was a shit head. But he was a fun shit head. He was our shit head.

I am going to spare you the details. It's really not fun to write about, this book isn't about sexual assault, and I know most of you have your own awful experiences so I don't really want for this to trigger anyone. All I will say is that Ben thought it was a bad idea for me to spend $30 on a cab ride home by myself when I could just walk over to his apartment a few blocks away. As I quote, "You're basically my sister."

If that is not the most psychologically twisted last line you have ever heard in your life then I don't know what is. I don't remember much, but I do remember saying no. And frankly, that's all that matters.

I remember thinking legally I was totally screwed. My father was a lawyer and I knew from the get-go that my case would have been a nightmare, especially back then. But you know what, even today it's hard to get a rape conviction, especially when the victim has a relationship with the perpetrator. My only defense was my word against his. And I wasn't emotionally strong enough to put myself in that situation. Not that I have to defend my choices.

It was clear to me that therapy was a necessity at this point.

I had put it off for too long, which is ironic considering my career path, but it was time.

The first few sessions were a bit awkward, as is expected. My therapist was soft-spoken and patient, and I wondered if she judged me. Were my problems not enough? Were they too much? Was I disassociating because I could talk about it without crying? Was I processing in the "right" way? Did she think I was a complete idiot for putting myself in a dumb position? Did she know, too, that I should have known better?

These are common thoughts we all have when in therapy. It's part of the process.

As I patiently waited for my ah-ha moment, I came to really like therapy. Partly because I really liked her, but also just because it was good to talk about this with someone who didn't feel the need to cry over what happened. I didn't feel like I was burdening her or dragging her into some personal mess she wouldn't be able to get out of. It was clean. And it felt healthy.

And then, my ah-ha moment came. And it was just as beautiful as I had hoped it would be.

"Kali, a few years ago, I lived in a safe neighborhood. Every day around lunchtime, I would go and walk my dog around the block. I wouldn't lock my doors, because, like I said, it was a safe neighborhood. I took a longer walk than usual that day and came back to find my house robbed. I was so embarrassed. As the police arrived to get my statement, I told them it was my fault. I had left the door unlocked. I had been careless. The police instantly responded—you did not ask for anyone to rob your house. I would recommend locking your doors in the future, but you cannot take fault for this. Just because your door is unlocked does not give somebody a right to come in."

In one story my therapist had freed me from a voice that burned inside of me every day: I should have known better.

Game changer. And not just with sexual assault—with everything.

Transitioning from childhood to adulthood is complicated. As children, we don't protect ourselves from danger. Our parents do. We don't think about guarding ourselves or taking necessary precautions other than putting on our bike helmets or buckling our seat belts. We run free. We have faith that everything will be ok.

But at some point in our late teens or early twenties, that changes. People hurt us. Jobs decline us. Failure consumes us. And violates our boundaries and dignity become far too common. As children, we would simply ask questions for clarification and lean on our parents for support.

But as adults, "we should have known better."

It's a message we hear from other adults, and from ourselves. We harbor the guilt and the shame and the embarrassment for getting dumped, or for not getting the job, or for putting ourselves into an unknowingly dangerous situation.

And this is the cause of the quarter-life crisis. We are desperately trying to balance freedom, enjoyment, authenticity, vulnerability and innocence with armor, responsibility, expectations, and accountability. It's a constant battle between blaming ourselves for almost everything, while still clinging to our childhood optimism that we are special and everything will be ok if we continue to work hard.

But the good news is that at least I understand. I've been there. And no matter what it is that you are struggling with right now, it's legitimate. You don't have to be a sexual assault survivor in order to feel the confusion that comes with transitioning into adulthood. You don't have to know what it's like to not get the job you really want or to be dumped by somebody or have your parents go through a divorce.

The quarter-life crisis isn't about the events that happen to us in our early twenties, it's about the self-doubt we feel as we slide closer and closer to adulthood.

Yes, it's destructive. But it's also curable.

I crawled out of my quarter-life crisis determined to make something of myself. But all I could really think about was you. I cringed at the thought of anyone else feeling like I did for those three years. And who better to help you get out of the chokehold of the quarter-life crisis than someone who won the war herself?

So once I finally left the garbage behind me, I started my own business that crushes the quarter-life crisis. And not only has it helped hundreds of girls across the world move forward with their lives, it also moved my life forward, too.

It even gave me the freedom to support my fabulous and near-perfect boyfriend (now fiancé!) who quit his lucrative job in the middle of his own quarter-life crisis. Because again—nobody is immune to its power, and nobody deserves to be miserable. Not even lawyers.

I hope this book helps you make better choices, accept greater challenges, and reminds you that you are capable of creating a fabulous life.

I'm here for you.

3

Symptoms of the Quarter-Life Crisis

Ok, so you know what defined my quarter-life crisis, but what about everyone else's? You might not relate to every beat that I went through during my twenties, so I want to make sure you are aware that the shitty feeling you have right now in the pit of your stomach is DEFINITELY the quarter-life crisis.

So let's talk about it.

If you really think about it—the requirements of growing up are rather egregious. We go from eating late night pizza and cheap beer while studying a few hours a day (if that) for classes that typically don't matter to being a full-blown adult.

We're supposed to get a job that pays us a decent salary (good luck), live in a Pottery Barn-esque apartment with our equally successful friends, keep our slim physique that's been battered and bloated from late night pizza and cheap beer, and in the meantime we have the haunting realization that this is the start of the rest of our adult lives.

If we don't get our career path, our relationships, our friend-ships, or our success right now—*will we ever?*

HOLY $&*# THAT IS A LOT OF PRESSURE.

The reality is, this is one of the biggest transitions you will ever face aside from marriage and parenthood, so act like it. It's ok if you don't swing it out of the park on your first shot. In fact, you won't. And for the people don't skip a beat during this phase—I'm honestly a little worried for you. I'd rather have you get the shit beat out of you while you are still young and resilient.

If you aren't totally sure if "quarter-life crisis" is the most accurate description of the hell you are currently experiencing, I've compiled some classic warning signs.

1. You hate Sundays.

Ah, the 'Sunday Scaries.' That itchy, antsy, uncomfy feeling you get when you realize *tomorrow is Monday.* Monday is not good. In fact, Monday is never good. Monday means you have to go to the job you hate. Or stay at home figuring out your next step while your friends go to work. Maybe it's the harsh reminder that the real world is calling your name, and you are desperately trying to ignore it. But whatever Monday brings—you do not like it one bit.

Typically, if we hate Mondays, it's not really because we have to get up early in the morning. I mean, that sucks, don't get me wrong, but that's not really it. If we truly hate Mondays, it's because we are unhappy with how our week plays out. The weekends are great—we get to escape the constant fear, anxiety, and nerves that adulting brings—but Monday pushes all of that aside and makes us face our reality. Yes, I'll admit that it is normal for most 20-somethings to hate Mondays. But the degree of hate might not be.

Be honest with yourself and think about the level of anxiety you get every time you realize Monday is approaching. Ask yourself why you hate it so much—and if you could envision a time in your life where you don't hate Mondays. If you are really feeling the effects of the Sunday Scaries, then you are definitely in a quarter-life crisis.

2. Visualizing the future is difficult.

Where do you see yourself next week? What about six weeks from now? Six months from now? Two years from now? Can you be specific? Really dive into what you visualize for yourself. Describe your job, your relationship, your living situation, and your trajectory.

This is a rather exhausting activity, isn't it? You don't like me very much right now. (I still like you.)

Humans naturally like forward progression. We like to know we are going somewhere. It doesn't matter if you're a planner or not—we ALL feel better when we have some sort of clue as to what our lives will hopefully look like in the future. That's why we save money. That's why we wear sunscreen. That's why we eat healthy (errr...or try to). We like having our future selves back and planning on what would make us happy down the road. So if we feel like we aren't going anywhere—well that can be a mood killer—and a major side effect of the quarter-life crisis.

Don't worry—drawing a blank, or even the polar opposite: having extremely grandiose visions of the future—doesn't mean you are royally screwed. It just means you have gone through a lot of change in a short amount of time, and setting realistic goals within a general direction is a daunting task. You're overwhelmed—another key factor of this phase in life.

3. You feel like time is against you.

Everyone has that moment in time—that scary realization that they have reached the age where they thought they would have their lives figured out. Mine was 27. That was a fun birthday.

It's truly frightening. All of a sudden, time is a big deal. Before, it felt like time couldn't pass us by faster! We wanted to drive. We wanted to vote. We wanted to drink. And after all of that…we still had some years left to experiment in a socially acceptable way. But then…24 hits. 26 hits. 28 hits. 30 hits (#29Forever). Whatever your number is—it's arrived and flying by rather quickly. And quickly, this anxiety about being "old" attacks with full force. You feel like you are actually running OUT of time instead of having too much of it. And the panic starts to set in.

Breathe. You might be behind schedule in your eyes—but I promise, you still have time to figure everything out. It's just important to not lean into any more "throw away" years and really focus on what it is what you want. And I can guarantee you one thing—your timeline won't look like anybody else's. And that's totally fine.

4. You "should" yourself.

It's a natural phenomenon. We freak out about getting older. Anxiety ensues. And without question, the should-ing begins.

I should have a boyfriend.
I should have made money.
I should have a better job.

I should be able to support myself.
I should be happier.

It's so cruel. So, so cruel. We had this imaginary life planned in our head when we were 16, and for some reason, we just can't let it go when 26 rolls around. Where is our fairy tale life?! Where are the money and the love and the accomplishments we swore we would have by now?

You were a successful teen. You made the grades and socialized with friends and were liked by your peers. Most people didn't worry about you going on and accomplishing something wonderful. You didn't really worry about it, either. Why would the rhythm of your life ever change?

Because adulting is freaking hard.

The semi-good/semi-depressing news is, our decade old expectations probably weren't even realistic. And more than likely, we didn't have concrete goals set in place to reach them. Hell, I wanted to win a Grammy by the time I was 18 and I figured the Tooth Fairy would drop it off at my front door. That seemed like a very plausible situation for my 11-year-old self. Everything else seemed to fall right into my lap (including money under my pillow), so why wouldn't one of the world's most cherished accolades? Totally reasonable.

This Grammy desire was clearly not the crux of my quarter-life crisis, but I'll bet it had something to do with it. It's healthy for us to dream, to plan, to fantasize. The problem arises when we reach adulthood and have the rude awakening that life isn't handed to us. We didn't *fully* expect it to be, or at least we will never admit that, but we did expect our magic touch to follow us throughout adulthood. Instead, we proceed to beat the shit out of our self-esteem because we couldn't construct our expected life.

Our lives should look different. At least, that's what we keep telling ourselves. This constant bully we have in our minds just won't let up. Our life is never good enough. Small victories are taken for granted, and it's taking its toll.

5. You get anxiety on social media.

Man, I miss the days when Facebook was fun. Don't you?

We posted pictures of what we did on the weekends, wrote on each other's walls and commented on funny articles. I would say things like "OMG I miss your FACE" and other borderline creepy things to some girls I really didn't know that well but pretended to know super well. Good times.

But now Facebook is just a big fat picture of what we're missing out on. Everyone is engaged. Or married. Or pregnant. And while you are happy for them, you're also wondering when the hell things will start happening for you.

And let's not even talk about the Photoshopped beautiful selfies, brand new Mercedes shots, exciting job announcements, and my personal favorite, #blessed.

Barf.

Social media has become a place where you confirm your own self-doubt and insecurities—not a place of mutual sharing and excitement. It's a cesspool of comparison, not a celebration of friendship. I think at its core it's meant to be a platform of connection and sharing, but not for our generation. We are stuck with the one-upping, trolling, over-exaggeration of successes, and the rat race of adulthood.

It's not like we feel good about it, either. We truly wish we could scroll through the photos and feel genuinely ecstatic for our peers. We wish we also had good news to share so we could chime into the excitement, too. Of course we look forward to the day where we can go online and share our own accomplishments—but for some reason, nothing seems good enough to post.

And that's probably because you don't want to feel inauthentic. But remember, perception is not reality, and social media is **not** the beacon of truth. We all cope with the unpredictability of life in different ways. Some like to project the essence of control so they can convince themselves they are actually in control. That's a reasonable coping mechanism. The problem with it is that we put too much weight on the veracity of these posts. So just keep that in mind as you move forward.

6. You want to change something big.

Enough is enough. You're over it. You're tired of feeling sorry for yourself, you're tired of feeling left behind, and you're tired of not having any answers. Wallowing is the worst, but man is it easy to fall into.

The problem is that you're not exactly sure what to change, or how to change it. It's really hard!! Quitting your job is scary. Finding a job is not as easy as you'd think. Meeting someone new is intimidating. Saving money can seem impossible. But something MUST give because you can't stand this funk for much longer.

Good. So let's keep going.

7. You have NO idea what your timeline should be.

Ah, the pinnacle of adulthood. Looking around at everyone else and wondering, "What the hell am I doing?" Isn't it rude that no one ever answers you? Haha jk. They don't have an answer, either.

I think I've determined the general reason most of us feel this way after graduation: our timeline vanishes. Sure, we hold onto that fairy tale timetable that we made up when we were sixteen. You know, the one where we decided we were going to be married, own a house, a couple of dogs, make six figures a year AND have the white BMW 5 series all by the time we turned 26. (lol)

Back then we had a full decade to make all of that happen, so it seemed totally plausible. But now, as I mentioned earlier, we've learned adulting is much, much harder than it looks. Bye, bye 5 series. Hello, student loans and sky-high rent.

So when should we have everything figured out? When *should* our fairy-tale life start being a reality? Welp.

Life would be so much easier if we knew when things are going to start cookin' for us. It's easy to have a day marked on the calendar that represents when your life is officially "together." But life doesn't work like that. Growing up isn't a project you have to turn into your teacher for a grade. It's organic. It's a process. And it doesn't have an arbitrary 'start' or 'finish' date. So you get to make of it what you'd like. And you don't have to feel pressure to 'get it together' immediately. In fact, you can flounder for as long as you want if you feel like you're heading in a good direction.

8. You're struggling between "have to" and "want to."

So, here are some realities about adulting:

You have to pay the rent.
You have to eat food.
You have to pay taxes.
You have to have health insurance
(for real or else you get fined).
You have to pay for gas or Ubers or bikes or cabs or what-
ever to get your butt around.

Yeah. It sucks. But you hafta.

But what if you hate your job? Or you hate your apartment? Or pretty much everything? Eeesh.

One major problem with the quarter-life crisis is struggling with the distinction between obligations and unnecessary evils. The truth is, adulting doesn't mean being miserable. But it does involve adjusting to a lot of new responsibilities. Yes, you have to have a job that pays the bills. But that's all—you don't have to have a job you hate. There are plenty of ways to make money. And the best part is, more than likely you have way fewer responsibilities now than you will in five, ten, or fifteen years. You can wait tables, drive for Lyft, nanny, work retail, or do a lot of other things that allow you to spend time working on projects you love. As long as you are covering your obligations and bills, you're good.

Yes, it's good to set a great foundation for yourself. But is making money really the only way to do that? Of course not.

Plus who's to say honing your special talents and spending time doing more untraditional things (think: traveling) won't pay off in the future? You are a living, breathing investment. So treat yourself as such.

The other plus side to this adulting thing is that it also comes with the power to choose how you spend your time. So once you go through your obligations—rent, groceries, insurance, gas, loans, debt, and any other miscellaneous necessities—you get to decide what you do for the rest of the day. Strapping yourself down with a million obligations is no way to live life. You are allowed to enjoy your life even if you haven't made it yet.

9. You have to figure out your finances.

Sooo along with paying the bills and handling your obligations, you also have to decide what to do with the rest…which can be daunting. Do you spend the money on some exercise classes or a night out on the town? Does your bonus go towards a new outfit for work or bottomless mimosas at Sunday brunch? Decisions, decisions.

You've heard this before: sometimes you gotta spend money, to make money. So where you spend your money has a pretty big influence on how you enjoy your twenty something years.

Now, you don't necessarily have to invest every dime you have into something that will make monetary gains. Like we mentioned before, this isn't all about money. But it is important to invest your money into yourself in order to get a return on your happiness.

So draw a circle right now, and start segmenting off the areas where you spend your money. Make sure the slices of the circle represent the overall percentage of how you spend. Come up with categories such as clothing, entertainment, loans, bills, rent, food. Look at the breakdown. Do you like what you see?

If you aren't spending any money on things that make you a better version of yourself—that is another sign that you are having a quarter-life crisis. Not being in control of finances is a big no-no.

So ask yourself, where is your fitness budget? Your physical health budget? Your mental health budget? (hi!) Your education budget? Are you actively investing in who you are as a person and your overall happiness? Yes, with adulting comes budgetary decisions—but make sure not to ignore yourself in the process.

10. Keep a solid support system.

The struggle is beyond real.

Maintaining our fabulous friendships that we did such a good job cultivating in high school and in college for some reason seems borderline impossible the second we start to properly adult. Where does our time go? Where does our energy go? Where do our friends go?!

It is brutally important not to isolate yourself during the adulting years. It might feel like everyone else is totally owning this whole adulting thing—but you'd be surprised how difficult this time is for everyone. And wouldn't it be nice to have someone to bitch to who totally gets it? You know it.

It's understandable you're tired after work. You don't have the energy to make the phone call or join the happy hour. Plus money is tight and plane tickets are expensive! Allowing your friendships to slip doesn't make you a horrible person—but it does put you in a rather compromising situation.

11. You deal with relationship pressure.

So let's say we actually start dating. Like, for real. We meet someone we actually like, IRL, and we start dating.

Woof. What pressure.

It was easy to not take dating too seriously in high school or college. That was the time to experiment, find out what works for you, and meet new people. You knew the chances of meeting someone you were going to marry at that age were probably rather slim.

But. Now…you are kinda taking it seriously. Eeek.

It's not like you necessarily want to get married tomorrow, but your grandmother would sure appreciate it. So you're caught between understanding that you're too old to be dating jerks, but perhaps too young to settle down with the white picket fence and a couple of labs in the suburbs.

And let's say you haven't met anyone yet. Oh, girl. I feel you. Being single is a BLAST in your twenties. But at a cost.

There are the fun questions such as,

Why aren't you seeing anyone? You're so cute!

The setups.

I have a friend who has a pulse and a job. I'll set you up.

And the accusations.

Well maybe if you focused less on your career and more on your hair, you would bag a babe.

All the while you might semi-enjoying being single, why is it anyone else's business? And why do you have to defend yourself for your choices?

The fact of the matter is, **you are going to be under relationship scrutiny from here until the day you stop caring.**

That is the reality. If you are single, people are going to be wondering why. If you are in a relationship, people are going to be wondering when you are getting engaged. If you are engaged, people will be wondering when you will be getting married. If you are married, people will be wondering when you are going to have children. And then, you get to cash in your relationship pressure for parenting pressure.

But luckily, that's not my wheelhouse.

4

Let's Vent

Contrary to popular belief, venting is healthy. It allows you to exhale the negative so you have a shot in Hell to at least recognize the positive. Ignoring or suppressing icky feelings only causes you to get wrinkles and look constipated. At least that's what I've heard.

Chances are a lot of the advice you've received has been "push through" or "when I was your age…" or "stop complaining and do something." Thanks again, Karen. Supes helpful.

So let's bitch and moan for a second, shall we? This is the space to do that. You have been holding in this desperation, this agony, and this fear for too long. So why don't we all take a deep breath and let it all out?

Here's why being a part of this generation not only sucks sometimes, but it also creates the perfect environment for a fugly quarter-life crisis.

1. We are always on display.

Always.

Our perfect parents got to join Facebook years down the

road when their lives were already settled, successful, and wrapped up with a pretty little bow.

That's not the case for this crew. We joined Facebook right as it was starting. Our friends and family have seen our *entire* adult evolution unfold online. Any inopportune moment ranging from a super embarrassing Friday night to graduating college without a follow-up "work" post is documented.

We have not been able to escape any poor decisions, any silly mistakes, or any downright irresponsible actions that we have apologized for over and over again.

Oh yeah, it's all on there. Before anybody meets us IRL, they can get the dirt on us from over 1,000 miles away.

Take relationships. When things fall apart, we inevitably have to ask ourselves the question, "How am I going to handle this on Facebook?"

(cue massive de-tag cleanse)

Being "in a relationship" on Facebook is the cyber version of a wedding ring. You're off the market. And when relationships end, knowing our entire high school class saw us get dumped might cause dramatic side effects, *Legally Blonde* style.

In summary, when things go wrong, we have to deal with it in in two parts. First, they lovely task of facing the music ourselves, and second, dealing with the social backlash. Which usually isn't that forgiving.

Just another day in the life of an over-exposed Millennial.

2. Dating is a joke.

Don't believe me? Even the *New York* Freaking *Times* says the dating culture is over. Hooking up is the new dinner and a movie, and I don't think any of us are really sure how to handle it. Yes, some may say due to the high divorce rate our cohort decided to handle romance differently, but we're not so sure if *this* is the answer.

At this rate, getting asked out on a date is about as rare as finding a job on monster.com. It just doesn't happen. (Unless you have in fact landed a job on monster.com, and then in that case you and I need to talk.) Dating might as well be called "boys asking girls if they like to cuddle via messenger." We have to BEG for romance, and even then, dates typically end up at bars with a group of people. Lame.

Honestly, it would be fine if we were prepared for this. And by now, a lot of you are. But I am willing to be that many of you were told lies and jibber jabber that prepped you for a dating-filled adulthood. Your parents probably met in college, right? Or maybe shortly thereafter? Your dad was nervous and pursued your mom for a while, she relented after a few dates, and they ended up together at some point. Maybe they are still together today.

So you went off to school thinking "YASSSS no more high school boys! I'm finally going to date!"

I mean, what a letdown.

It's not you. Of course it's not you. It's just that people are so accessible and inaccessible all at the same time. We get to know each other via chatting and sexting instead of over coffee or after work cocktails. Yet, we're expected to drop everything at 1 AM when a guy we've been chatting with for about two weeks asks us to come over and "watch a movie." Sex is arguably MORE accessible than going out on a date. How frustrating is that? You are expected to put out before you're even courted.

So, needless to say, dating is a definite joke.

3. We have *killer* expectations.

Yep, our expectations are ambitious. And lethal. All at the same wonderful time.

But just to get this straight, dreaming is good for us (for the most part). Think about it—we wouldn't have the *Hunger Game* series or the Uber app if we weren't acting on our creative impulses. For real, the city of Los Angeles would have no safe way to get home after a night filled with irresponsible drinking if it wasn't for Millennials.

We. Are. Awesome.

However, this "killer" is two-fold. The crappy part about our expectations is that we slowly die inside when things don't work out. Embarrassment and shame are our lovely version of death and taxes. And they have even uglier consequences.

A few of our favorites are cutting others out in order to dodge personal questions, comparing ourselves to anyone and everyone, and should-ing ourselves.

By now, we **should** have the dream job. We **should** have the boyfriend. We **should** be content. But we aren't. And what we SHOULD do is give ourselves permission to fail, and try again.

Easier said than done.

4. Divorce freaks us out.

You're talking to the generation where roughly half of us come from divorced parents (raises hand). So, while we're incredibly idealistic about our career pursuits, we're struggling to figure out how we feel about our romantic endeavors. And that, of course, comes AFTER we actually get another human to share a cup of coffee with.

If we believe whole-heartedly in love, then are we just asking for a divorce to throw us a surprise party in 20 years? If we decide to abandon the notion that love lasts forever, are we cynical and grumpy ALREADY? And doesn't that give us premature wrinkles?

It's all very confusing.

All we know is that divorce is a very frightening possibility that we would absolutely love to avoid. We didn't like dealing with it, or we didn't like seeing our friends deal with it. We need some time while we sort this out. We don't want to feel pressure to rush down the aisle. We know we're alarming marriage statisticians everywhere (is that a thing?), but nuptials are something plan to take super seriously.

5. We push boundaries.

When you combine high expectations with fear of conventions—it's only natural that many of us will create our own ways. We skip marriage. We're coming out. We change our jobs faster than we change our nail polish.

We are grasping every opportunity to take risks, break conventions, and figure out what works best for us. And we really have no reference point. Our parents took the jobs they had to take, and in turn, many are encouraging us to take the jobs we want to take. Believe us, we're beyond grateful. We're just faced with the paradox of choice, and we *definitely* don't always get it right the first time. With new boundaries comes new failures and we're willing to take the bad in with the good.

6. Limbo is the bane of our existence.

We are constantly in a state of limbo. And we HATE it. Nothing is ever certain! Our parents are retiring and moving away, the job market is impossible, if we can actually land a job it either isn't secure, commission based, or we're already planning an exit strategy, and our dang friends won't stay in one place. ICK! Many days, we feel stuck, hopeless, and confused. So, what's our next move, you ask?

Beats the heck out of us.

Limbo is an asshole, and nobody really seems to get it. We can't talk about it to our friends, because then we have to admit that we're struggling, and that's embarrassing. We can't talk about it to our parents because their reference point is a bit skewed. So usually we sit and stew on it ourselves, which normally consists of us thinking ourselves into a black hole of doom.

So what are we going to do about it?

We're going to cure it. We're going to fight for ourselves and fight for our future. We're going to get out of this rut no matter what.

And I'm going to help.

Part 2

Career

I realized in all the cases where I was happy with the decision I made, there were two common threads: Surround myself with the smartest people who challenge you to think about things in new ways, and do something you are not ready to do so you can learn the most.

—Marissa Mayer

Find out what you like doing best and get someone to pay you for doing it.

—Katherine Whitehorn

5

Career and Personality

Another big factor of the quarter-life crisis probably has to do with the fact that your job sucks. Or that you don't have a job. Which depending on how shitty some of your jobs are, not having a job may or may not be even worse.

On the conservative side, we spend 40 hours a week at work. But let's be real, the majority of us spend more like 55+ hours of a week at work, and ideally 56 hours a week sleeping (I am including naps because you are not sleeping 8 hours a night, bad girl). That leaves 57 hours of free time per week. Mind you—that time is split up between showering, cleaning, traffic (ugh), cooking, organizing, prepping, and exercising.

Yikes.

This is why it's pretty important to have a job you at least tolerate. I know a lot of you don't necessarily need to find your heart's true passion in life in order to enjoy working. I agree, and this is coming from someone who started their own business.

Every job is going to come with its bullshit tasks you don't want to do. I hate doing pretty much anything other than writing and coaching so if I'm honest with myself, a good chunk of running Blush is doing a bunch of stuff I really don't like. SO, I get it—you don't have to love every aspect of your job in order to be happy. **But you can't hate it.** It just takes up too much of our time.

So, how do we go about *not* hating our job?

Unfortunately, I can't go into specifics. I have no idea what kind of job you have or how toxic your work environment is. I don't know if your boss' crazy assistant is storing her mother's pee samples for her doctor's appointment later in the day in the community fridge and you're supposed to look the other way. (Yes, that has actually happened). But I can help you figure out the best jobs for your personality.

Bear with me, I'm about to get research-preachy on you for a sec.

Although it might seem like common knowledge that personality and career are obviously linked—that wasn't the trending belief for a long time in the United States. Due to wars, the Great Depression, and societal pressures, many believed that work was an obligatory endeavor necessary to keep food on the table and contribute to a bright future for offspring. Careers were far from being held as an avenue for individual expression.

However, psychologists over time began to develop models and theories that educated the public on how career and personality are inextricably linked. Holland's Career Codes, Roe's Personality Development Theory, and most notably, Carl Jung's personality theory that was later developed into the Myers-Briggs Typology Indicator test have all been popular modalities for individuals to sort through the various careers available and see which one fits their temperament the best.

I tend to favor the Myers-Briggs Typology Indicator exam,

and many of you probably already know your types. If you don't, you can take the quiz here.[1]

Just for reference, when you take this quiz, I don't want you to ask yourself, "In a perfect world, what would I do?" or "What SHOULD I do?" Instead, just face the facts and answer what you actually do in typical situations.

For example, if I were to be asked the question, "Do you like closing deals with a handshake or a contract?"—the "ideal" me would want to answer "with a contact." I know that contracts are in place for a reason and that responsible people use them. But if I'm being honest with myself, contracts are super boring and I would rather assume that everyone is a nice person and a handshake totally suffice…and this is why I surround myself with lawyers.

Also, just a quick warning, once you do know your type, you are in severe danger of becoming addicted. I am 100% not sorry about this.

Ok darlings, let's see what careers for your personality type fit you best.

Extrovert Types

ESTJ—"The Boss"

The name says it all. As an ESTJ, you prefer to be in charge of your work environment. You do your best when you can manage, coordinate, delegate, and drive other people to achieve goals. You prefer structure—and lots of it—and don't mind stepping in to create organization in the workplace. ESTJs work

1. http://hello.joinblush.com/personality-quiz1

best with other people—alone time only drains your energy and doesn't inspire you to be better. You love taking on responsibility and you are a fabulous decision maker. Practicality is also a must—you need to see real impact, and you would prefer to see it yesterday.

Take away: stick with leadership. The more you can delegate, orchestrate, and direct—the better off you are. Make sure you have ample control in your chosen field so you can continue to feel motivated.

Ideal Careers: Finance, Business Management, Supervisors, Military Officers, Leadership Positions, CEO, Strategy, Operations

Stay away from: Lots of alone time, little control, subjective fields (arts, humanities, social sciences).

ESTP—"The Negotiator"

Known for your practical yet flexible ways, ESTPs need a variety of stimulus to keep you going. You prefer objects to ideas and don't mind getting your hands a little dirty to get a job done. You can be a ruthless negotiator (you go, girl!) and can change tactics on a whim to seal the deal. You're adaptive, high energy, and flexible nature allows you to play many different roles with people in order to achieve a goal. You need action and flexibility in order to achieve your full potential. No deadlines. Little structure. Lots of action.

You're going to work in a high energy, fast paced, and intensely social environment. Constant phone calls, emails, meetings, and negotiations are right up your alley. Teamwork is always going to suit your social butterfly tendencies!

Ideal Careers: Talent Agent, Mechanic, General Contractor, Marketing, Sales, Athlete, Litigator

Stay away from: Cubicles, strict deadlines, routine, the arts.

ESFJ—"The Guardian"

This personality type excels in caring for others. You do best when you can guide, teach, and help others around you. Like the ESTJ, you are going to do your best when you're in charge, but instead of a knack for strategy and logistics, you possess a certain warmth and personable quality. This essence makes you extremely favorable with others and allows you to be in charge of many at a time. People can't help but want to follow your lead. ESFJs prefer to see the practical impact of their work and like to see measurable improvement from others. You thrive on structure, group settings, predictability, and clear expectations.

Your favorite feeling in life is to feel appreciated, so make sure you work with a team who understands the amount of energy and effort you put into your career. Being around other caring people is going to make your life much easier, so focus on the environment you are walking into and make sure there is room for your loving leadership skills!

Ideal Careers: Teacher, Social Worker, Health Care Administrator, Hospitality, People Leadership Skills, Coaching

Stay away from: Working from home, blurred guidelines/expectations, lack of impact for others.

ESFP—"The Traveler"

Novelty is key for the ESFP Traveler. You need new people,

new experiences, new tasks, new EVERYTHING. Routine is a bore, and you will do anything in your power to stay away from it. You are great at getting in the action and diving right into the work. You have an affinity for others and for animals, and enjoy being in practical fields. You can adjust very easily to new situations, and prefer to operate without a clear agenda. True to your name, you enjoy bouncing from place to place, taking it all in, and transforming your experiences into something tangible and relatable for those around them.

Spontaneity is going to help you flourish so try to avoid doing the same thing every day. Different hours, different environments, different people—it doesn't matter. Just make sure to change it up. And remember—your positivity is contagious. Never doubt your ability to turn around a sluggish office into a 24/7 party zone.

Ideal Careers: Travel guides, Performers, Artists, Animal care, Teacher, Fitness Trainer, Consultant, Sales

Stay away from: Data entry, admin work, lengthy academics, routine.

ENTJ—"The Director"

Clocking in as the highest paid personality type, the ENTJ knows how to intersect creativity with business. Similar to the ESTJ, you do your best when you are in charge (and can help innovate). You prefer structure and thrive in organization but need to feel connected to whatever endeavor you are chasing. You like to "drink the Kool-Aid" and you go all in whenever possible. In an ideal situation, you can combine your creative instincts and good taste with your ability to lead others and make sound business decisions. But without the creativity element, you can feel suffocated and directionless.

When looking for a job, think creativity meets business. You're going to be about strategy, innovation, trends, and profits—which is why you are such a great asset to companies. But remember—sitting alone in an office is not going to do anything for you. For you, teamwork really does make the dream work.

Ideal Careers: Entrepreneur, Chief Executive Officer, Producer/Director, Organization Builder, Sales, Marketing, Operations

Stay away from: Lack of creativity, individual work, little room for innovation or development.

ENTP—"The Innovator"

Almost like a jack-of-all-trades, you are going to be happiest when you can use your talents to create solutions, develop innovating strategy, and offer insight for better results. Like the ENTJ, you need to be creatively attached to whichever career you choose. Project development is always going to be a home run because your mental muscles can be fully utilized. Like the ESTP, you are extremely adaptable and can excel in a range of different careers. And, because of your extroverted nature, you excel better as a team member or a leader.

Innovating and creating new strategies, concepts, and solutions will always be a highlight of your career. Make sure your job gives you the freedom and space you need to create something that has an impact. And if it needs to be a group effort, the more the merrier!

Ideal Careers: Corporate Trainer, HR, Marketing, Sales, Consultant, Community Organizer, Strategy, Operations.

Stay away from: "busy work," lack of influence in strategy formulation, working from home.

ENFJ—"The Muse"

Altruism is the name of the game with the ever-lovable Muse. ENFJs feel a deep need to help others, create impact, and to do so in a creative and energizing fashion. People are your language—the way they feel, what inspires them, and how to tap into inner talents. You highlight others' talents and foster creativity and inspiration, hence your name. You like leading others in a pursuit of creativity and prefer structure to organize your days. But, without meaning and impact attached to your career, you will lack the joyful satisfaction of a hard day's work.

Focus on helping others in a creative fashion when looking for a job. If your talents can be channeled to help anyone—whether that's a large group or a few individuals—you will feel connected to the universe and enjoy your career on a much deeper level.

Ideal Careers: Counselor, Teacher, Social Worker, Public Relations, HR, Real Estate Agent

Stay away from: Lack of impact in helping others, lack of creativity, unstructured work environment.

ENFP—"The Romantic"

With more thirst for opportunity and more talent than they can handle, the ENFPs are drawn in so many different directions it's hard to pick just one. You love the spotlight, are incredibly creative, and sustain high energy levels through being surrounded by others. Your attention span is a little low—meaning you prefer a fast paced work environment with constant new challenges for you to face. You also love finding ways to help others—but in a more spontaneous fashion. The challenge will be in finding a career that caters to your spontaneous nature. Ideally, you should find a job that offers a wide range of duties to keep your focus.

Your flexibility allows you to travel for work or to have different hours on a daily basis. You are great at meeting and connecting with new people and performing has always been your strong suit. You are naturally inspiring, so leading others on a group endeavor is a great use of your talents. You can be happy in many different fields, but that's the beauty of it. So focus on the people and the activity level—those two are going to sustain you above all else!

Ideal Careers: Performers/Actors, Entrepreneurs, Counselor, Writer, Teacher, Advertising, PR, HR.

Stay away from: Authority, structure, busy work, little room for growth.

Introvert Types

ISTJ—"The Enforcer"

Reliable, practical, hard working and loyal, the ISFJs value long and stable careers. Due to your respect of tradition, you might find yourself drawn to well-established fields. You flourish in routine (do not ever let yourself sit around and do nothing!), and you do your best when you can control exactly how your day unfolds. You are self-sufficient and hard working and do not need any team members to motivate get your butt in gear. And once you make a decision to see something through—they do so with perseverance. Needless to say, employers LOVE you. I mean, who wouldn't?

You are going to thrive in a career that pays close attention to detail and incorporates a sense of duty. Your loyalty and dedication to social values make you a great candidate for government or medical positions. But don't let that deter you if you aren't into science or politics—your work ethic and a sharp eye will always make you a great candidate in any field.

Ideal Careers: Accountant, Auditor, Lawyer, Surgeon, Economist, Police/Military Officer, Detective, Editor, Stockbroker

Stay away from: Instability, unpredictability, subjectivity, and large teams.

ISTP—"The Engineer"

...Otherwise known as Curious Georgette. As an ISTP, you are constantly curious about how things work, how to offer practical solutions, and what's next in the day. You thrive on unpredictability but still remain practical in your endeavors. You learn best "hands on" and bore easily with abstract theory. You need freedom to wander and explore—or else you will feel stifled. Your introverted nature gives you the ability to concentrate, which comes in handy when needing to solve problems. Your talents vary all over—but you will do best without the confinements of routine, structure, and authority. Which is why many ISTPs don't enjoy school. No worries, it's normal.

No matter what field you are drawn to, make sure that you are involved in the construction, building, or the creation stages. Your talents make you a prime candidate for using tools in order to create something wonderful—and that's also what is going to make you feel the most fulfilled at work. Focus on creating and you'll be right at home.

Ideal Career: Police/Detective, Firefighter, Computer Programmers, Engineer, Mechanic, Carpenter, Pilot, Athlete

Stay away from: Strict hours or rules, spontaneity, mindless busy work.

ISFJ—"The Philanthropist"

The ISFJs beautifully combine two amazing skills together—people and organization. You are in tune with others' wants and needs and have a rather fabulous gift of being able to organize systems, operations, and products in order to fit people's needs. This is going to allow you to do well in a variety of different careers—although most ISFJs do tend to gravitate towards one that value stability. As long as you can stay within a practical world in order to see a visible way to create impact, you're going to be just fine. Service is your jam, and your job should honor that.

It's good to note that your personality time is arguably one of the most versatile personality types of all the sixteen. You have strong social skills even though you are introverted, are able to be flexible even though you prefer structure, and can still "the big picture" when organizing the small details. This might be challenging to find a job that you LOVE because most jobs will fit your skillset—so try to focus on helping others above all else. This is what will make the biggest difference in loving your job!

Ideal Careers: Nurse, Designers, Veterinarian, Dentist, Decorators, Child Care, Social Work, Doctor

Stay away from: Immeasurable work, disarray, harsh criticism, lack of service.

ISFP—"The Artist"

More than just a job, you as the ISFP search for more of an overall calling. You like to use your hands to connect with the world in order to find purpose. Creative freedom without confines is your ideal scenario. This might mean that you will stray away from the traditional corporate world, and that's totally fine. You focus on staying in the present and making your current environment a beautiful sanctuary. To you, structure is mundane and organization is limiting. You are a free spirit and need to experience new surroundings in order to feel fulfilled! Planning ahead isn't quite your thing, so the independent contractor relationship tends to appeal to your spontaneous eye.

The biggest takeaway is finding the ability to create beauty to share with the world. This is where you will always shine.

Ideal Career: Artist, Photographer, Cosmetologist, Designer, Massage Therapist Musician, Teacher, Writer

Stay away from: Abstract ideas, deadlines, long-term commitment, routine.

INTJ—"The Iconoclast"

Fiercely independent and original, the Iconoclast is known for breaking down incredibly difficult and abstract theories and converting them into realistic solutions and strategies. You prefer working alone and strongly value autonomy. You need space so that you can be creative with your original problem-solving.

You are analytical in nature and value structure in your work. Busy tasks are definitely not your thing, and you normally try to find shortcuts to work around it. Authority is also on your bad side—but in order to execute your creative ideas, you sometimes need permission, which can become frustrating. Networking and small talk really are not your favorite, and because of this, you can feel alone at times.

The more independent you are within your career, the happier you will be. Finding a job that values autonomy and has a hands-off approach will suit you well—especially if you can be in on strategy and logistics.

Ideal Career: Scientist, Military, Lawyer, Strategist, Computer Programmer, Medical and Technology fields, Entrepreneur

Stay away from: Micro-managers, busy work, zero tangible results.

INTP—"The Professor"

The Professor thrives on being unique and original—which is perfect considering you only make up 3% of the population. You are extremely independent, abstract, eccentric, and non-conformist—which means the suit and tie gig probably isn't going to pique your interest.

Logic is your language, and you love to analyze abstract ideas and philosophize over various theories and proofs all day every day. You love to innovate, in fact, fellow Professors have been the source of many scientific discoveries throughout the years! The INTP has an entrepreneurial spirit at heart, and your introversion leads you to do research independently. Competition just does not motivate you, girl. And, neither do practical solutions—but abstract projects can hold your attention for hours.

Ideal Career: University Professor, Technical Writer, Engineer, Scientist, Lawyer, Consultant

Stay away from: Non-project based work, lack of theory and logic, competition.

INFJ—"The Prophet"

The Prophet is a rare breed—making up less than one percent of the population—but your impact makes up for their small numbers. You are passionate, creative, and insightful, and use your idealistic and optimistic nature to create concrete steps to help impact the lives of others. You tap into your compassion and strong will to help others help themselves, and feel that their life should have meaning and purpose.

It is good to note that you have an abundance of empathy, and you can sometimes get swallowed in others' emotions. Creating boundaries in your personal life and at work will do you well. But without able to exercise this empathy and create personal connections to others and to their work, you can feel lost, so it's best to focus on people-centered work.

Ideal Career: Screenwriter, Blogger, Counselor, Life coach, Spiritual Guide, Healthcare, Clergy

Stay away from: Busy work, little connection to work or purpose, high conflict.

INFP—"The Poet"

Out of all the personality types, you are going to have the hardest time finding a job you love. But once you do find it, you NAIL it.

You might find yourself caught between rejecting the idea of long schooling and lusting after careers that require additional training. So, you typically do best when school and work are linked inextricably to a core value. You prefer the written word to all else, in fact, many young Poets dream of becoming accomplished authors. Luckily the Internet has opened up many methods to connect with others through writing.

Do your best to avoid those entry-level sales positions. You might like people, but you definitely don't like selling to them or working with them on a constant basis. You need project-oriented work and space to be creative. Don't shy away from going out on your own—our introverted and flexible nature will keep you focused.

6

Quitting Your Job

Now that you know what job best fits your personality, you might be looking at your current job thinking "Ahh, now I understand why I feel like I've been suffocating in my own misery for weeks on end."

But you don't want to be a quitter. You should be grateful for the few stable parts of your life, right? While everything else is going down the crapper at least you have consistent paychecks to hold you afloat.

I get it. Quitting your job feels irresponsible, bratty, and entitled. You think it's what gives Millennials a bad rap. We have too high of standards and whine all the time. That's why everyone hates us.

But you know what? Haters gonna hate. I love being a Millennial. Seriously, I really do. And you know why? Because of people like you. Because you want to do more, feel more, and be more. You want to reach your full potential and contribute your very best to this planet. And you know what? You've decided you can't do that at this job.

So quit.

Please don't spend one more day punching your iPhone

awake at 8:15 AM praying that it's already lunchtime. Quit making excuse after excuse—*well my manager isn't that big of a dick, I really like getting 25% off at the downstairs restaurant, I guess I'd lose my AT&T corporate discount...* No. Just, no.

No more waiting for the next promotion or bonus or reasonably tolerable day. You can't afford to waste your life away doing something you hate. You are creating the foundation for the rest of your career RIGHT NOW. So if this job isn't cutting it, then let's start finding something new.

If I haven't convinced you enough yet, here are some big fat warning signs that it's time to quit your job.

1. You aren't excited about the next step.

Or any of the steps afterward, either.

Take a look around you. There is at least one person, if not plenty, who are above you in status. You probably interact with them on a daily basis, or at least hear about them on a daily basis. So by now, you have a pretty good idea of exactly what it is that they do.

The question is, does their cool fancy job excite you? If so, that's a good sign. That means there is hopefully room for growth and exciting possibilities ahead of you continue to stick it out. If not, what are you doing?

Room for growth has to be one of the most motivating incentives for staying at a company. Period. People work hard in order to have a pay off for their future. We save money so we can spend it later. We eat healthy so we can look and feel good later. We put in the hours at work now so we can get a promotion later. So if the prospects of the future positions at this company are not enticing to you, what is your motivation?

Humans need to feel like we are going places. Forward movement is a necessity. So if you don't feel like moving forward in the company because you aren't excited about what's at the end of the tunnel, get out and find a place that excites you.

TL; DR: No room for growth = no room for motivation.

2. Your job doesn't fit your personality.

Remember that whole part on the Myers-Briggs personality stuff? Did you think about your current job and if it fits with your personality type?

If it doesn't, you are walking into an uphill battle from the get-go. You can't change your personality, but you can change your job.

3. It's all about the paycheck.

Yes, it's good to have money. I won't argue that. But when your paycheck is becoming toxic to your health, we have a problem.

If you are staying around just to collect that comfortable lump sum every other week, there are lots of other ways to make money. Ways that won't crush your soul. And let's face it, in the end if your unhappiness and stress continue to increase, you won't be around to enjoy all that money you've been collecting anyway.

Point is, **do not let money intimidate or imprison you.** There is a lot of it out there, and there are plenty of ways to wrangle it in. So what if you need to wait tables for a handful of months to get by while you figure out your next move? At least you will feel like you're actually heading somewhere exciting rather than withering away in a stale cubicle.

Never let money be your Hello Kitty Band-Aid on your infection prone axe wound when your job is beating you down. It's just not worth it. So start researching ways to make some fast cash to cover you during your transition phase, and let's keep going.

4. You continue to compare your career to your friends' careers.

Sure, the grass is always greener on the other side. Or is it?

I find that most people who are truly happy with their careers aren't looking over their shoulders wondering what their peers are up to. It's just like owning a dog. When you truly love your dog (which most decent humans do), you don't compare your dog to somebody else's dog. You love your dog. Your dog is special. In fact, your dog is damn near perfect. So who the hell cares what Rover is doing next door when you've got little Emma curled up at your feet? Not me, that's for sure.

Same goes for careers. If you feel like everyone else around you is doing something that seems more worthwhile, it's time for you to give yourself the chance to explore other options. This deep insecurity that is causing you to compare your job to your friend's jobs is only going to get worse if you continue to ignore it. Bitter and cynical is not your style. So instead of holding onto this resentment, find an alternative. Get excited about your life again. Find a goal that makes you proud of yourself.

If you can do that, you'll never feel a twinge of career jealousy again.

5. Your job dissatisfaction is spilling over into your personal life.

This is really important. If you are so unhappy with your current career that it's affecting other areas of your life, you have got to make a change.

Have you ever heard of the story about the boss who yelled at the man who then turned around and yelled at his wife? Then the wife yells at the kid and the kid kicks the dog. Poor dog.It's a pretty terrible story with a major moral at its center: stress affects your life and the people in it in more ways than you are even aware.

Do not let your shitty job cost you your happiness. It is not worth it. Careers at their worst bring in money for us to live off of and supply a mildly pleasant way to spend our weekdays. At their best, they fulfill a core need of ours to influence our environment and contribute our talents to society. And BONUS—they also pay the rent and then some. Meaning, your career can be an amazing source of happiness. And for all the hard work you have put in thus far to receive an education and land a job, you deserve that experience.

7

Unemployment

Ok, so some of you are really annoyed at me right now because I've been writing loads about quitting a terrible job that you don't even have. (But would probably like to just to give you a sense of purpose!) I'm sorry! I know. Salt, meet wound. It stings.

Unemployment is terrible. Just, terrible. It stirs up the absolute worst in us. It brings out our anxiety, boredom, frustration, and even despair. We lose faith that we have anything to offer society. Did we trick ourselves into thinking we were actually worthy of earning money in exchange for our skills? HOW DID THIS HAPPEN?????

panic

But I know that you know that's not true. Unemployment can play tricks with our minds and convince us that we're never going to make a living, no matter how hard we try.

Just to refresh your memory, when I graduated from college, I applied to upwards of 100 jobs and heard back from one—a few months ago. Then, when I graduated from graduate school and MOVED to a new city for a private practice job, I was promptly fired for wanting more clients.

So. Yeah. I'm a bit of an expert in this field.

Don't let this sucky phase question your capability. Trust me, you ARE worthy of work. You are worthy of doing something great. And if you can just hang on a little longer, you're going to be just fine. But in the meantime, it's good to be as productive and positive as possible so you can at least enjoy your break and create a foundation for later success. So here are some tips for you during this yucky transition period:

1. Cast a wide net.

Part of the problem when facing unemployment, especially longer gaps, is our tendency to operate under tunnel vision. We get fixated on ONE job, ONE specialty, or ONE skill. But the reality is, we are good at a lot of things. We can perform well in a lot of environments. And we work well with a lot of people. The more opportunities we create for ourselves, the better our chances are of moving past this unemployment phase and moving into adult life. You are only making it harder for yourself by chasing a limited amount of opportunities due to fear or insecurity.

Do not talk yourself out of applying for a job because you think you're not qualified. That's not your decision to make. That's the company's decision to make. So cast that net as wide as you possibly can.

Put yourself up for as many positions as possible. Because in the end, you can adapt. You've been able to learn from dozens of teachers, work well with handfuls of different people, and make friends with groups from all over. So you'll be able to adjust to whatever life throws at you. Just give yourself a chance and keeping fishing.

2. Keep an open mind.

Again, don't let your fixation fool you. You might have studied Public Relations, but I'll be damned if you aren't turning out to be a marketing pro! Maybe you buried yourself into psychology books, but management is looking super tempting right now.

All of that works. You don't have to follow the linear path. You don't have to chase what you studied in school. In fact, you can pursue whatever the hell you want as long as you get pumped about it. Give things a chance. Consider the fact that your life might not turn out how you'd always thought it would. No one's ever does! And yours might turn out to be better than you ever expected if you open your mind up to the possibility that you are meant for something you never even considered to begin with.

Pretty exciting, eh?

3. Volunteer.

Feeling completely stuck and have a lot of time on your hands? Give volunteering a whirl. Not only can volunteering give you the inside peek into what a potential job is really like, but it can also fulfill your feelings of purposeless for the time being. I wouldn't recommend volunteering full time, though. You have bills to pay! Money to save! But a part-time volunteering gig will take your mind off the limbo, satisfy your desire to contribute, and educate you in a new field. And who knows? Maybe a part time volunteer job could turn into a full-time paying job that you love. Yay opportunities!

4. Use Plan B.

(No, not the kind you get at the drug store.)

Ok. So. About dem bills.

They can't just disappear. It's fine if you're receiving financial help from parents or family—totally normal—but don't write yourself off from being financially capable. Instead, go for Plan B. What can you do in the meantime that will pay? Yes, a full-time job that you absolutely adore—with benefits—would be nice, but we are already searching for one of those. So what can you do in the interim?

Ideally, you want something that produces quick cash, has minimal training, and naturally has high turnover. This way you can get in and out whenever you do finally land a job you love.

I've had plenty of interim jobs in my life. I've worked in admin, retail, food service, babysat, and even done accounts payables (that was rough). All of these were inherently short-term positions that filled in the gaps between school or job slumps. And dang did they do the trick. I was busy, making money, and not drowning myself in the misery of the unknown. Plus, I wasn't spending money while I was working. That in itself was worth it.

My favorite job out of the bunch was bartending by a mile. It was perfect. I made a lot of money, was able to get my own apartment, and had flexible hours for school. I could have easily sat around and eaten bonbons until I graduated, but forget that. I was hustling.

However...

I also had to wrestle with my own disappointment in myself. I didn't want to be working at a restaurant—my dream was to grab a job in the counseling field so I could gain some real experience and join my friends in the 9-5 working world.

I just wanted to feel like a grown-up. I can tell you with confidence that my dream definitely wasn't to serve drinks for people I went to college with who accepted their pomegranate martinis with condescending eyes. ("All that education and she ended up here…?")

That was not Plan A. Hell, it wasn't even Plan F.

But this job taught me more about customer service, quick decision-making, management, and business than I could have ever hoped for. I still to this day wonder whether my masters in counseling or bartending for Hillstone prepared me more for running Blush (true story). Plus, that job also kept me on my feet, introduced me to some good humans, and taught me how to make exceptionally fabulous cocktails. Win-win.

So spring for the Plan B. It could be more beneficial to you in the short term than a "real" job could be in the long term.

5. Communicate.

You don't have to do this all on your own. Pump your network. Vent to friends. Lean on mentors. Cry to your family. Just do something! Don't let yourself wallow or stress or let your mind go in circles all by yourself. Get others involved. Not only will they help you gain perspective, but they can also put the word out there that you are looking for a new opportunity.

Remember, in order to get what you want, you have to ask for it. And sometimes it helps to have others ask for it, too. Communicating about your uncomfortable situation might be nerve-racking, but just one conversation could spark an opportunity that you hadn't considered before.

It's also good to surround yourself with positive people. You need to feel empowered. Uplifted. Excited. Optimistic. Nobody wants to hire someone down in the dumps—so you've gotta make sure you are taking care of your emotional health.

Part 3

Friendships

If friends disappoint you over and over, that's in large part your own fault. Once someone has shown a tendency to be self-centered, you need to recognize that and take care of yourself; people aren't going to change simply because you want them to.

—Oprah Winfrey

One friend with whom you have a lot in common is better than three with whom you struggle to find things to talk about. We never needed best friend gear because I guess with real friends you don't have to make it official. It just is.

—Mindy Kaling

8

Bad Friends and Bullies

You are who your friends are...or something like that.

It's not fun to admit this, but a very large chunk of the quarter-life crisis stems from our friend choices. I'm aware that I might come across as a proud flake when I say this, but I'm going to say it anyway.

Many of our friendships serve a temporary purpose in our life. When we were in elementary school, a lot of our friends were our friends because they lived down the street. In high school, we paired off with people who were in our same clubs or classes. In college, we gravitated people who also happened to like cheap beer and costume parties.

As adults, we tend to make friends based off of common experiences. For example, two friends might meet each other because they are both struggling through tough breakups and need some support from an understanding source. Some might bond over the horridness of their boss or the stress of the job. Some might become besties through planning a wedding simultaneously.

Though it's fabulous when these friendships stay in tact once the common cause expires, a lot of times, they don't.

For example, let's say you meet Karen when you are in a very Eeyore state of mind. Your mood is so sour it puts Jolly Ranchers to shame. Karen is your salty equivalent, so the two of you find solace through bitching and moaning to your heart's content. It's a match made in hell. One day, you decide you are tired of feeling sour. You find ways to reconcile your gawd awful mood and start to feel more positive about life again.

So...what happens to salt-show Karen? Ideally, unless you pledge to wear headphones during her bitch-a-thon, you probably move on.

I know, I know. It doesn't seem fair, but in a perfect world, you would decide to start putting your positive attitude first and leave Karen to decide if staying negative is really worth it. You would understand that by keeping this friendship alive, you would be gnawing away at your emotional health.

But that's not how it normally plays out. Instead, what actually happens is you choose to stick around because you feel bad. You put expectations on Eeyore Karen to start acting like a Piglet when in reality you should be spending your time trying to find other Piglets to play with. It's not fair to poor Karen and it's definitely not fair to you.

This is why we tend to have an "oh shit" moment in our 20s when we look around and think, "Where the hell did everyone go? And who are these terrible people that managed to make the cut?"

You held onto the Eeyores while others went off to find their Piglet. It's a harsh realization, but if you are not actively sorting through your friends on a yearly basis (at least), you are going to be susceptible to some questionable friendships.

During your quarter-life crisis, you cannot still be saddled with your party friends who truly believe anything can be solved with a dab of crystal light in our vodka water. You can't be surrounded by people who are threatened by every little thing that you do. And people who legitimately think the world is out to get them definitely can't support you. Ya can't.

But you probably are. And therein lies the problem. Having bad friends during the quarter-life crisis is like going to battle with a troop that's half asleep. You don't want to be in the trenches with people who don't have your back. I know that it's easy to romanticize friendships that last a lifetime—especially friendships from high school and college—but prioritizing a fantasy over your wellbeing isn't a great place to grow from. We have to acknowledge the realities of our social group and make sure that they are setting us up for success, not making us second-guess ourselves every other step we take.

Do not forget that friends, no matter how old we are, have a huge influence on us—even if we are out of those impressionable teenage years. It's no surprise that plenty of successful business mentors advise younger protégés to hang out with successful peers.

Why? Because success breeds success. It's the same line of thinking as "never be the smartest one in a room" or "guilty by association." In fact, I like to be the dumbest person in the room. It's actually scary how easy it is for me to orchestrate that, too…but that is an entirely different conversation.

Anyway, the people you hang around have more of a role in our lives than we think. They become the norm for us. They are our baseline of what relationships, family, careers, work ethic, and success look like. So no, it's not JUST going to happy hour here or shoe shopping there—this is the very basis of what you think healthy human interactions look like. Your friendships define what your normal means.

This ain't no drill. This is real talk.

That is a huge amount of responsibility to be placing on people that might not be up for the task. You may have some friends who want to stay Peter Pans forever, but frankly, you don't have time to be their Wendy. You have shit to do.

So does that mean you have to cut out everyone from your life who borderline sucks? Ideally, yeah. But if you're not one for confrontation or you're scared you might not have anybody left standing, I understand. Kind of.

So right now I want to focus on what poor friendships look like, how to handle those situations, and tips on "how to find your Caroline." Aka, how to find the best human friend in the world. (I personally think she's more of a Tigger than a Piglet but I will let it slide. And yes, I'm probably more of a Pooh. It's a sad realization that I just have to accept.)

So let's get to it.

I'm going to list out descriptions of all the shit heads you're probably dealing with right now, and hopefully you can recognize a few.

1. The Convenient Bad Friend

This is the friend you have whose friendship is completely on their terms. You probably only see them when it's convenient for them. It's not that they don't like you. You're a delight. They just don't prioritize you. At least, not to the same degree that you prioritize them.

These are the people who will typically call you when they are super bored on a Monday night and no one will play with them. Maybe their boyfriend is only out of town every other week and that's when you get a guilt text. Or, even worse, they will call when they need a ride to the airport last minute. These are ALWAYS the people who forget uber exists.

They also totally ghost on you when their "normal crew" is around. If they were featured on a sitcom with five other leads, you would be Gunther pouring their coffee. [insert poop face emoji]

It's probably not an everyday bummer, but always feeling like an extra isn't great for your self-esteem. Out of habit, you probably feel like you have to cater to this person—but you don't. Even though you would really enjoy feeling like part of the ensemble, you don't wait in lines. Not when it comes to friendships you don't.

I genuinely don't think that these friendships are based on disrespect or mal intent. I really don't. More than likely you are very well liked and respected amongst this friend.

But does that matter? Not really. Not when you feel broken hearted every time you see an Instagram pic of the gang sans YOU on Friday night. You didn't get the invite. And although your house party of one is banging, it stings not to be invited.

So instead of being a silent accomplice to this self-destructive friendship, you need to reassess your friend prioritization. Make time for people who would drop anything and everything to take you to the airport last minute, even though you would never ask. (BECAUSE DECENT HUMANS UBER.)

It's best to shove their prioritization down the toilet and meet them where they're at. If you're bored on a Monday, then go hang. Why not? Win-win. But you are no longer going to vie for someone's attention when you're cool enough to hang by yourself. Your expectations for this friendship will tank, and inversely so, your happiness will rise.

2. The Negative Friend

This one is difficult. You really like this girl. She's there for you all the time, she genuinely cares what you have to say. Overall she *seems* like a good influence.

Except for one tiny thing. She never has ANYTHING positive to say. Ever. The sky is always falling. You can try giving her advice, but it will fall on deaf ears. You can try listening to her with all your might, but she never gets enough out of her system. And at some point you have to wonder, are you this person's friend, or are you their counselor?

Let me tell you this right now: never provide free therapy. You are actively taking money out of my pocket and I am going to get you for it.

But in all seriousness, counseling is actually tough work. Listening to someone actively for a full hour while also thinking on your feet and coming up with solid, foolproof advice? Yeah, I'm going to get paid for that. And if that's what your relationship looks like with this friend, your rate should start at about $75/hour. Follow my friend the Joker—"if you're good at something, never do it for free."

Yes, I am aware I just quoted a villain but you know what, he has a fucking point.

I think the hardest issue when it comes to these types of friends is that being negative isn't a crime. Your friend doesn't deserve to be shunned from the world. But, she might not deserve all of the quality time you're putting in because unfortunately, she's influencing your way of thinking. And she's taking advantage of your patience.

Anyone's life has the ability to look really awful or really awesome, it's just a matter of perspective. And if you want to see your life with rosy tinted glasses, then it's probably best to surround yourself with other people who drink the happy Kool-Aid.

Plus, if she doesn't stop with the Eeyore vibes, she's gonna bum you out for good. You'll end up resenting her and turning into a bitter cynical 2.0 version of her. Then people will start isolating themselves from YOU because you've picked up on some Debbie Downer habits.

TL;DR: You are enabling a negative little monster who is going to gobble up all of your serotonin and spit it out in the garbage can.

Don't do that. Talk to her about how her negativity is affecting your psyche, and if she doesn't stop, then help her find a professional who will listen. And if she refuses to help herself, then resist the urge to rescue her. Your friendship will be closed for business. Otherwise, you're only reinforcing her negative behavior, making you an essential part of the problem.

3. The Super Lazy Bad Friend

These are definitely my favorite of all the shit friends. They always are down to go out, hang out, or chill out. In fact, they are pretty much down to do anything except work. And as much as we all love this friend, we have to recognize that they might not be challenging us as much as we need.

To be fair, it's totally not their job to get our butts moving, but sometimes they can rub off on us in ways we don't want. Remember—success breeds success, and if we constantly surround ourselves with people who really don't feel like pushing themselves to do anything other than drink beer every night of the week, then the chances of us pushing ourselves to do anything else plummets.

Another symptom of constantly hanging out with the fun lazy friend is that you start to question your own motivation. Why ARE you working this hard? DO you take everything too seriously? SHOULD you just loosen up? Maybe life IS just about having fun all the time?!?!

Nonononononononono. No. You are you because you care so much. You are reading this book because you care. You are actively thinking about your future because you care. Yes, it has its ugly side effects (namely, the quarter-life crisis) but it's also such a wonderful quality to have and it is going to carry you through this mess. Don't start to shame your caring gene. And don't let anyone else make you question it, either.

Instead, try to find others who care. If you find friends who take their lives as seriously as you do, the bunch of you are going to be motivating each other and lifting each other up, instead of encouraging you to skip the workout or not worry about updating your resume.

I promise you don't have to ghost on these lazy friends. They can be the absolute best. Just monitor your time with them and make sure you aren't mimicking their behavior. You are an ambitious little booger and I want you to stay that way.

4. The Ego-Driven Friend

Blah.

This girl just CANNOT deal with the fact that you might have something wonderful going on in your life! So, in order to support you, she just has to share something even BETTER about her wonderful existence.

It's a shame, really, because she has the most hilarious sense of humor and can really bring light into a dark situation. But friends need to support each other and have a give and take. And you deserve time in your friendship to celebrate your accomplishments, especially when they feel so few and far between.

As annoying as this is, big egos are typically created via low self-esteem. If this girl means a lot to you, be honest with her. Tell her that this behavior comes across as if she's not happy for you. Because for goodness sake, it's not like you've been shouting from the rooftops about how brilliant your life has been lately. Things aren't working out like you thought, so we have GOT to make sure that you are giving props where props are due! When you score big, I want your bestie to be smiling so hard her cheeks bulge into her earlobes. But more on that later.

Just watch out for the friends who have such delicate egos that they can't seem to muster up any happiness for your successes. Friendships should operate from the heart. They should be filled with vulnerability and love and respect and appreciation.

The ego is an ugly place. It's insecure and volatile and defensive. It's never happy for anyone else and gets upset at the smallest slight. So if you recognize a large ego in a friend, be wary, because she doesn't have the capacity to be emotionally supportive for you.

6. The Mean, Bad Friend

Now, she's not a bully to you. No way. She's super nice to you. You two hang out all the time and get along famously. In fact, you actually didn't even know she was a mean girl for a while.

Sure, your other friends mentioned a few times that they didn't LOVE her, but she has a strong personality. Maybe she's just not everybody's cup of tea. It wasn't until recently that you started to notice, dang, she really isn't nice to other people!

Maybe she started pointing at strangers and laughing at them for their attire. (If you want to borrow my retort, it's typically, "I own that in pink...!") Maybe she openly was rude to a friend at a house party because they wore shoes in the house accidentally. But what's probably the most likely is that she just got comfortable enough with you to really start talking some mad shit about other girls in the group.

Not good.

Whatever happened, it sucks when you realize your friend is mean. It's up to you whether or not you want to continue being friends with her, but know that

- If she's a bully, chances are people will think you are, too
- You are just encouraging the behavior by giving her the positive feedback of being her friend

and most of all...

- If she does it to other people, chances are she will do it to you, too.

Pick your poison.

5. The Needy Bad Friend

Chances are, you only hear from this girl whenever a crisis is happening. They hardly ever check in when everything is good and well—they only need you when shit is about to hit the fan.

It's flattering sometimes. You are a great mediator and an even better listener, so you can offer good advice, a few well timed jokes, and some perspective in order to help her feel better about the little mess she has created for herself. You give her the time and attention she needs to heal, and you even let yourself get excited that maybe this catastrophe has given new life to your stale friendship.

And then she totally ghosts. It'll be another six months until you hear from her. So, you have two choices. Be there for her when she needs it but don't expect anything in return, or stop indulging her and positioning yourself yet again as a severely underpaid counselor.

If you are getting a confidence boost from these sporadic engagements, I'll take it. It's nice to feel needed and if you aren't feeling totally neglected and abandoned when she finally does heal herself and moves along with her life, then I don't see much harm in this. But eventually you might get tired of this act, and that's when you are going to have to set a boundary.

Author's Note: Now is a good time to take a silent inventory on how many crappy influences you have in your life at this given moment.

At this point, you might be realizing that you have some pretty terrible friends. In fact, you might be downright panicking. *Big breath in through the nose, out through the mouth.* And you're also probably realizing that a lot of your problems could easily be stemming from your terrible network of awful humans.

So I'm going to take it a step further. A lot of those friends mentioned above aren't necessarily bad people. They probably don't realize the pain they are causing and ideally the dynamic could be fixed with a few honest conversations.

If you want to keep the friendship in tact because you genuinely think they have such fabulous potential, by all means, talk it out. Be honest and straightforward and let them know exactly how much this current dynamic is hurting you. But there's another batch of friends that I am going to tell you to do away with immediately:

Adult bullies.

Adult bullies are real. They are not some kid from an '80s movie wanting to steal your lunch money, and they aren't Regina George clones demanding their friends to disavow hoop earrings for life.

No. They're just normal people who have developed some sick coping mechanisms. And you have to suffer from it.

Unlike popular belief, bullies don't always "grow out" of their meanness. In fact, some people actually grow into their meanness and trade in their physical manipulation for emotional manipulation.

I've encountered many an adult bully in my life, and they aren't always easy to identify. My hysterical fear of confrontation paired with my soft determination to always be liked invited adult bullies to walk all over me for years. It wasn't until I reached my early twenties that I decided to free myself from people who didn't truly care about my feelings or overall well-being.

It wasn't dramatic. I didn't fight with anyone. There was no "it all falls apart" in Act III. It was mostly an organic unfolding of fizzling out. Most of these adult bullies don't even realize I view them as an adult bully (or maybe they do now thanks to this ridiculously personal book). But you know what? It's not my job to be the behavior police of womankind. I have a life to live. My job to take care of myself. And I want the same thing for you.

So here are some quick ways to spot whether or not you are associating yourself with an adult bully, and tips on how to handle them.

1. The Silent Treatment

How to Spot It: A classic tactic by almost all adult bullies. You have a foot-in-mouth moment? Silent treatment. You forget to text when you say you were going to? Silent treatment. You talk to someone else without them knowing? Silent treatment. You walk outside and smile and breathe in fresh air and are having an amazing day and seriously no one could ruin it for you?

Silent treatment. No matter what you do, eventually you will be met with their silence. Which also happens to be called emotional abuse.

They won't actually *tell you* what you've done wrong. That's way too much to ask. Instead, they will smoke you out with their lack of communication until you break. Nobody likes to be ignored, and silence is typically the best way to "beat" someone without actually having to put yourself out there. It's a cop out. Which is why it's so popular amongst adult bullies.

These types of bullies don't actually have the courage to get in your face. They would much rather have you do the dirty work for them. You get to torture yourself about what you could have possibly done wrong while they sit and sip their iced coffee across the way and wonder how badly you have spiraled out of control.

Then, they'll probably turn the tables so quickly, that a leg might actually slap you in the face.

Kali: *"Hey, did I do something wrong?"*
Karen: *"No, oh my God, what would ever make you think that?"*
Kali: *"Ok, it just seems like you've been a bit distant lately and I wanted to clear the air."*
Karen: *"I think it's all in your head. You tend to think everything is about you."*
Kali: *"Uh, ok. Yeah, I guess I do that sometimes. Hey, wanna grab coffee later?"*
Karen: *"I don't know, I'm kind of in a rush. Plus aren't you like super busy with that important thing you never told me about?"*

Editor's Note: If you are named Karen, I deeply apologize for not being creative with my fake names and I am sending you lots of love and light for your name abuse in this book.

I'm sure a lot of you got pretty pissed at Karen when she immediately jumped to a watered down version of: **"you're crazy."**

Why? Because you probably experience this on a daily basis. It's the oldest trick in the book. Girl calls someone out for behavior and is thanked by a sweeping accusation that she is in fact, crazy. **This is also called gaslighting.**

They'll blame your "crazy conclusion" on your hormones. Your sensitivity. Your selfish nature. Your lack of understanding. The fact that you have a vagina. I mean these people will find something, anything, to discredit your sanity. The best of the bullies will use a piece of information that they know you are already sensitive about. Good luck if you've been complaining about cramps—your period is about to buy them an out for their abhorrent behavior.

So how on earth do we handle something like this? You have one of two choices. You can either:

Call out the behavior immediately with full awareness that they might try to gaslight you. Let them know that you do not appreciate the silent treatment and you would rather talk it out at their earliest convenience. To be honest, many bullies will melt in the face of actual confrontation. They're great behind screens, but not so much in person. You calling them out might just be enough to break their behavior (with you) for good. If they do in fact gaslight you, your energy does not need to be wasted. This person is being manipulative, abusive, and incredibly disrespectful. And you are being really fucking mature for even having the guts to call them out in the first place.

So walk away. Tell them that you aren't going to argue with them and that the conversation is over. Do not let someone control your emotions. You know what you saw, you know how you feel, and that's all that matters. Convincing them isn't your job—you already did the brave thing by communicating.

Or you can just ignore them.

If this person really isn't worth your time, let them go. I like to tell clients all the time that having the tough conversation is great for relationships you want to hold onto. But if this person sucks (and you need to come up with some FABULOUS arguments as to how they do not), why go through all the effort when you know you don't want to ever see them again? Your energy is precious and it should not be wasted on a wanker like that.

If you feel like you are doing them a disservice by not being honest with why you are flaking, then, by all means, be the Good Samaritan and let them know. But afterward, get the F out of dodge and make yourself a promise to never indulge or reinforce their behaviors ever again.

2. Isolation

How to Spot It: By the time they reach adulthood, bullies have long concluded that victims are more malleable and impressionable when they are **alone**. So one of their most dangerous and effective tactics is to isolate their victims so that their punishment and behavior digs much deeper in the future.

Isolation comes in two forms: they will either manipulate scenarios to where you create distance between yourself and others, or they will actively tear you down so that others create distance from you.

Both have disastrous consequences. The easiest way to spot this behavior is when a new person introduced to your life simultaneously brings tension with others. It's like whenever someone walks into a room and all of a sudden you smell a nasty ole fart. It's not guaranteed that the newcomer let it rip, but it would be a rather unlikely and unfortunate coincidence.

It is true that healthy cliques fall apart every day over legitimate reasons and it has nothing to do with the debut of new friendships. But more than not, the tension is introduced because your new friend doesn't want you to have other friends—and that's to their benefit. When adult bullies decide to control your behavior, it's exponentially more effective if you don't have a support system waiting to set you straight. You're on your own—making their behavior tactics much more impactful.

If you suspect there is an external force driving a wedge between friendships you value, act against it. Make sure you are doubling down on your outreach. Talk about the tension and make sure you are clearing up any and all misunderstandings that might be circling around your social group. Do not brush things under the rug and hope that they will "blow over." Be proactive with your friendships at all costs.

If you are starting to feel unsatisfied with your current friendships but can't point a finger as to why, evaluate it. Carefully. Don't let one person define your relationships. Support is crucial for handling adult bullies—so try to keep as much padding as possible.

3. Walking on Eggshells

How to Spot It: If you feel like you are tip-toeing around a friendship: certain topics are off-limits, activities have to be done behind their back, or you have to omit or conceal certain information as to not "rock the boat"—then you are walking on eggshells.

Oof. Isn't that feeling just the worst? At any given moment, something you say will set off an explosion of death stares and nasty quips. You feel like you can't be your true self because your true self is either offensive, undesirable, annoying, narcissistic, nerdy, or simply not good enough. So you hide things and carefully maneuver the relationship so you can remain on good terms and somewhat enjoy yourself. But it's exhausting. You are doing so much work to keep someone happy who doesn't even appreciate the entire tapestry of YOU.

If you are playing a version of yourself to appease somebody else because you feel obligated to do so in order to dodge punishment and sustain the relationship: **you are friends with an adult bully.**

The only way to appropriately handle this is to stop with the act. If there is a theme to your tiptoeing, put it out in the open. Come clean about what you are concealing and why you are doing it. Maybe there's a chance this friend isn't as virulent as you think and they deserve a chance to see your authentic self. If they respond with punishment—namely, the silent treatment, then you know what you're dealing with. And thanks to Item #1, you also know how to handle it.

4. Lowered Self-Esteem

How to Spot It: Remember that bomb Halloween movie about the three witches? With Bette Midler and Sarah Jessica Parker and someone else. *Hocus Pocus!* Yes. Ok, remember how Sarah Jessica Parker and company suck the actual life out of children so that they can all stay young forever??!?

Well, that's what adult bullies do. Except they don't *technically* suck the life out of you. They suck the self-esteem out of you in order to keep *them* confident. In the movie, SJP likes to kidnap the youngest and most innocent children she can find, because that yields more youth for her to absorb. So in that same vein, adult bullies don't simply target insecure people—they **create** them. And the more self-assured, accomplished, and a likable person they conquer—the more confidence they can ride until they find their next victim.

There is nothing better to an adult bully than tearing away someone's self-esteem in order to strengthen their self-esteem.

This process comes in the form of insults, put-downs, back-stabbing, gossiping, and anything else that will peel layer after layer of the self-confidence you have been growing over the years. Their end game is for you to rely on them for any happiness you experience in your life. It's controlling, it's manipulative, and it's scary.

So if you are noticing a correlation between a friendship and a hit on your self-esteem, it's best to do some due diligence to make sure that this correlation doesn't actually mean causation. But sometimes it's really not worth finding out.

If you're game, I'd really like for you to end the friendship. Friends don't put friends down, and they *certainly* don't make emotionally rejuvenating meals out of them, either. If ending the friendship is not possible due to uncontrollable circumstances (think work, mutual friends, family), then keep this friendship at an arm's length as humanly possible. So long that your fingertips don't even touch. Protect yourself. Understand that you don't have to share things about yourself or be chummy-chummy or open yourself up to any potential breach. Put yourself first, don't let ANYONE manipulate your confidence, and suck the poison out of your life. This really just boils down to one thing:

This really just boils down to one thing:

Stop being friends with people you don't like.

And side note: if you are in a ROMANTIC RELATIONSHIP with ANY one of those people mentioned above, GET THE HELL OUT. The only thing worse than being friends with an adult bully is sleeping with one.

But back to the assumption that these were just your friends...

You are no longer in first grade. You do not have to invite the entire classroom to your birthday party so Karen's mom doesn't throw a hissy fit about her daughter's lack exclusion. We get to self-select our friendships and that might mean burying a relationship that's been toxic for YEARS.

Yes, there will be consequences. Things are going to get awkward and people may have some questions. But you know what? This blip of confrontation is going to be worth years of drama-free existence. You need a healthy environment for you to reach your full potential, and you don't need someone sucking it all away because they find power by putting others down.

So it's time. It is time to break up with terrible friends—bullies or not. In order to move forward, we have to let the dead leaves fall.

Let's get this straight: ANYONE'S level of influence in your life needs to be critically assessed. In other words: if they aren't bringing anything to the table, they gots to go.

Let the lecture commence!

In this life, there are promoters and there are demoters. *I know, I know. Cheesy AF but I'm being serious.*

Ok, so there are promoters and demoters. The promoters—you guessed it—promote you to newfound encouragement, motivation, enlightenment, happiness, optimism, and anything else that gives you the warm and fuzzies. They are entertaining and supportive. You want to call them when life gives you sour ass lemons and you want to call them when the sky finally rains sugary lemonade.

Demoters do just about the exact opposite. They make you question your success, your security, your ambitions, and your direction. They don't offer support when support is due, and you suspect there might be a quiet celebration when you struggle. Even if they are not a bad person in any way, shape or form

They don't make you want to be better. Being friends with them *takes energy away* instead of *providing it.*

Not everyone in your life is going to be a promoter. It's almost impossible unless you are Oprah Winfrey and only surround yourself with Super Soul Sunday goddesses. So yes, I'll admit that you might have a lot of 'neutrals' in your life who aren't bringing much in and aren't taking much away, either. But for those demoters who are causing more havoc than is justifiable, it's time break up.

I've given you the tools to identify which friends are demoters, but we haven't crossed over into which friends are the promoters.

So now it's time to find your Caroline.

9

Nurturing Positive Friendships

I'm so done with being negative. I think by now you've gotten the point: If they are a bad friend, ditch them.

So let's talk about ME.

I'm not one for having a million friends. I tried, though, for many years. I wanted to have all of the friends. The more friends I had, the more likable I would be. Right? I felt bummed out when I wasn't invited to every birthday party and desperately wanted to be accepted into any and every clique in existence. Even in college.

But then I learned something pretty shocking when I was 23. **I'm introverted.**

Ha! This whole time I had been going around and trying to be Suzie Sorority when all the while I actually was much better off having a few close friends I could rely on.

So before I launch into this, I want you to know that I am completely biased. You might be a bubbly extrovert with no intention to decrease your social circle, and you don't have to. But regardless of what personality type you favor, quality over quantity is always going to win when it comes to in-depth relationships.

And finding your Caroline is going to be a lifesaver.

So who is a Caroline?

A Caroline says "OMG that is AMAZING!" to every small accomplishment you do. She cheers for you when it feels like the entire world is stacked against you. She doesn't offer solutions to your problems; she trusts that you are smart enough to know the answers yourself. She reminds you that you are a badass fairy princess baller and that your life is going to turn out just fabulous. She always takes your side unless you are being a total bitch, which might happen from time to time. She takes your mind off the low points and focuses on the high points. But she makes sure to validate how you are feeling along the way.

Everyone needs a Caroline. Lucky for me, my Caroline is an extrovert. She has cultivated many amazing friendships and is well liked by pretty much everyone that meets her. Like, you would love her. Really love her. But even with all of her fabulous friendships, we have a special connection. And no matter how many other friends enter our lives, we have the reassurance that we will always be Caroline and Kali.

The reason I am so gung ho about you finding your Caroline isn't just because I live in my own little world and think my daily practices are the ONLY solution to living a happy life. (Though sometimes I can get like that.)

It's because this rough phase of your life isn't going to end overnight. This stuff takes time. You are going to have to heal, pick yourself up off the ground, find the motivation and the direction to chase, sustain your energy while you are grinding it out, and somehow land on your feet. It is a delicate balance that almost never ends. And I don't want you going through that alone.

Of course, there are professionals out there like me who are there for you during these transition years. Of course. But I want you to have something more than that. You have to have a permanent kinship that cannot be jolted by distance, anxiety, or circumstance.

I also believe that finding your Caroline is more about finding yourself than finding a great friend.

If you know yourself, like yourself, and are patient with yourself, then you will be open and secure enough to let another powerhouse female into your life. It takes confidence and a quiet ego to be friends with someone as amazing as a Caroline. If I was not consistently working on myself, then this friendship would all but destroy my sanity.

Carolines are super easy to be envious of, no matter when they come into your life. They are sweet and patient and kind and smart and steady. They are supportive even when their life takes a tumultuous turn. They are optimistic even when it feels like there's nothing to be grateful for. And they seem to go through life unfazed, even if we know that really isn't true.

Finding a Caroline involves tapping into your confidence and holding onto it for dear life. It means shedding any inkling to compare or compete. It requires the capacity to cheer for someone else even when your world is falling apart. You must tap into your vulnerability and let it run wild. Or else the friendship won't last.

But a Caroline is worth digging into yourself for because she will change your life forever.

If you are totally confused as to what a Caroline might look like, that's ok. I know this is a love song to my best friend, but I've found that healthy friendships all tend to look alike. There are common threads that make them so rock-solid and healthy.

So per usual, I listed out some traits that I have found to be omnipresent in every healthy friendship.

You laugh at each other's jokes.

Even if they really aren't that funny.

Good friends share the same quirky senses of humor. It's what helps your bond stay so strong. Plus, laughing at your friend—even when the joke was a bit off key—feels so natural. She's fucking hilarious to you, even if nobody else gets her.

Caroline isn't necessarily stand-up comedian funny, but her facial expressions and enthusiasm for just about anything are hilarious. I laugh at her storytelling, corny jokes, and offhanded comments all the time. Most of the time she's not even meaning to be funny. But that's what makes our relationship so great. We see the humorous side of everything.

Sharing the same sense of humor also ties together your coping skills. Humor is one of the most effective tools for gaining perspective. It breaks the tension and allows air to come rushing into life when you least expect it. Sharing that same rhythm of humor is essential to having an unbreakable bond. You guys don't have to have the exact same delivery, but as long as you can agree on what's funny (and what's not), you will be in sync.

There is no competition.

Friends. Do. Not. Size. Each. Other. Up.

There's no racing to achieve the next milestone first, and there's no twinge of excitement if one friend falls behind. Instead, best friends cheer each other on no matter where they are in life. They celebrate when things go really well, and comfort each other when they aren't.

Let me put it this way: Caroline found her husband, bought a house, got a job, and established a savings account all before I even woke up one morning. She has always been 10,000 steps ahead of me. But instead of getting angry with her for kicking my ass in life, she's encouraged and motivated me to be better. And I whole-heartedly embrace the challenge.

She makes me want to be a better human and do mature human things. She sets my standard of what "killing it" should look like. And somehow, she says I do the same thing for her. Granted I've asked her to Freaky Friday with me before and the hesitation in her voice makes me think otherwise, but I do think she's being honest.

It's important to note that good friends also don't shame each other for sharing good news or for feeling low when the other hits a home run (more on this later). They don't evaluate their life's successes based on the other's failings. Instead, friends enjoy the ride together. They understand that their pace isn't always going to match (welcome to my LIFE), and that's ok. It's the appreciation for each other's journeys that matters.

You both value honesty and trust.

Lying is poison to friendships. Just like in a romantic relationship, you have to have trust in friendships. There's no blabbing behind each other's backs, no sharing inappropriate secrets (especially to other big-mouthed friends), and there's no sugar coating the truth when you know that's what they are asking for.

Caroline and I keep so many secrets for each other that I think when one of us dies, the only source of solace will be that the skeletons in our closet were literally taken to the grave. That's how deep your commitment to trust needs to be. Honest enough to blurt out the secret truth, and trustworthy enough to never let it slip out.

This all comes from security within a friendship. In fact, the mark of a really amazing relationship is when both parties feel like they can actually be themselves, free from the constraint of politeness. Friends let each other relax and say what they mean without fear of judgment. And the more honest it gets, the stronger the relationship becomes.

You stick up for each other.

These friends aren't the two-faced kind. If anyone bashes their friend, they're ready to roll. Of course they aren't blind to each other's faults—we all have them—but it's not cool for anyone else to point them out, KAREN.

Not too long after John dumped me at the footsteps of the sorority house, Caroline happened to be invited to a party he was attending. And that night, John, silly, dumb John, thought it was a good idea to approach Caroline to have a bout of small talk.

Stupid, stupid, John. Thank God her now-husband was also in attendance that evening, or else Caroline might have punched him square in the jaw. As John reached in for a hug, witnesses tell me that Caroline's eyes got so big you could actually see your soul begging for mercy in their reflection.

Her arms glued to her sides, her nostrils flared up for war,

Caroline proudly yelled, "DON'T BOTHER" and hissed pure evil into his dumbstruck face.

Ah, I wish I could have seen it. John probably shit himself. Caroline don't play.

I truly believe Caroline wouldn't ever hit another human being, but if I were to make one exception for her, that would have been the night. And I totally know how she felt because I've felt the same way over people who have wronged her as well. And that's because good friends are a united front. They know they have each other's backs, and that's what makes life so much easier. They always have the reassurance that they aren't alone and that someone else understands them. And that is worth protecting from any outside threat.

You are invested in one another.

Best friends have met each other's families, significant others, and colleagues. They know all about each other's jobs, and what stresses them out and why. When they tell a story, there is hardly any background information to explain, because they already know the context. Why? Because they've been asking questions, listening to the answers, and participating in collaborative conversations since day freaking one.

Shelley, Caroline's mom, is one of my favorite people on this earth. She is feminist and accomplished and wise and supportive. What's not to like? And Caroline also happens to be a clone of my mother, Karil. We are quite the group.

I can't even tell you the names of a lot of my friend's parents, but that's because these friendships are special. We are invested. We listen to each other's daily happenings.

Good friends don't just dial in when drama happens—they

are there for the everyday, mundane, boring as shit instances that happen when humans exist from Monday-Thursday. They put the time in together, even if that means hanging out with mom once in awhile.

You normalize each other's experiences.

Best friends don't judge each other. They validate each other. They are each other's constant reminder that they aren't stupid, pathetic, or desperate for feeling completely and utterly lost during this confusing time of transition.

Caroline is constantly reassuring me that I'm not insane for moving to Los Angeles. She calms me down when Blush feels like it's too much to handle. She coaxes me through relationship spats and unnecessary LA drama. She's my pulse on reality. She brings me back to my logical self.

I cannot emphasize the importance of validating each other's feelings. Of making sure that your friend knows that whatever they're going through, it's okay. That they're not crazy. That their world won't end. That it's normal. This sort of friendship is our sanctuary—it's where we go to feel safe. The world makes us feel like we're out of our minds every day, but these types of friendships make us feel sane again.

You accept each other.

Quirks and all. Best friends don't wish their friend would stop doing this or start doing that—they just know that they are who they are, and they accept them completely. Faults and flaws become the trademarks of their friendship. It makes them human.

Caroline has like, an ultra weird obsession with her dog. She's so fixated on this little Maltese that sometimes I want to remind her that she didn't actually give birth to her. This dog is her life. When she was training her, Caroline would carry around a water bottle and spray the shit out of this dog so she would grow up to be a "good girl." I don't know how much it really worked but that is how dedicated she was.

A lot of friends would tell her to chill the F out and let the dog just be. But I think it's so funny. It's who Caroline is. Caroline goes all in. She loves this dog, and I love her for it. There's no resentment or wishful thinking. I'll take that Maltese any damn day if it means I get Caroline, too.

Always remember, asking their friend to be anyone other than themselves isn't really friendship at all. You gotta actively embrace your friend on a daily basis in order to create a safe place for each other to just be.

Now, as I mentioned earlier, when you find a Caroline, be prepared: **you might feel jealous.** Finding a friend so stellar does not come without consequences. She is going to be a trailblazer, and you are going to have to get comfortable with the idea that her life might take off before yours even approaches the runway. This is going to be especially relevant given that you are going through a quarter-life crisis. And it might be even more difficult if your Caroline isn't. She might be rocking into adulthood without a care in the world like mine did. In fact, her life might be hitting every single milestone you could have ever dreamed of (guilty). Then what?

You don't want to be that friend who can't be supportive and happy for her. That's not who you are. And as we have already learned, finding good friends is hard to come by the older we get. We can't afford to lose one of our gems!

So how do you handle a rock solid friendship when your friend seems to get everything you're wanting out of life? Well, for starters, you follow these steps.

Understand that your positive emotions and negative emotions are not mutually exclusive.

You can feel sad and happy at the same time. This does not make you a bad person.

You are allowed to acknowledge your sad feelings and express your positive feelings. You are allowed to recognize that her amazing news shines a little too bright on your shortcomings. And you can feel safe knowing that none of your sad feelings are chipping away at your positive ones.

Think of it this way: your two best friends, Katie and Karen, are both up for the same promotion. Both are qualified. Both are nice people. Both are deserving. Katie gets the promotion. You are very happy for Katie. You are very sad for Karen.

Now, does your sadness for Karen take away from your happiness for Katie? No. Of course not. You want to shout from the rooftops that Katie totally deserved this promotion, and you also want to cry in a corner for Karen because she didn't get an amazing opportunity she also deserved. **They are two separate emotions that are co-existing.** *Ok, I know, this might not be the most sophisticated or interesting metaphor you've ever read, but it still makes sense (fingers crossed).*

Once you can accept this notion, your guilt is going to dissipate. Once you allow yourself to feel all of the emotions at once, you will understand that they do not have to blend together. So you need not feel guilty about your sadness when you are genuinely happy for a friend. Your happiness can shine through regardless of whatever rainstorm is brewing within.

Remember that milestones happen in different orders.

There is no "right" order for how your life is going to unfold. And although you absolutely adore your friend and would love to be synced up with her pace, life doesn't work like that.

There is a very low chance you and your best friend are going to get engaged, married, promoted, pregnant, homeownership status, or anything of the liking at the same time. In fact, they probably won't even happen in the same year.

This doesn't mean that one of you is "ahead" and one of you is "behind." Because while she is out getting herself married, you might be working like a dog on your career. And a few years down the road, it might be your turn to get married while she is hustling her career. You both are going to get there. You're just not going to get there at the same time.

You didn't miss the boat just because someone else got on the early ride. You have plenty of time, and you don't have to keep pace with your friend, even if you love them. So remember that your life might be "out of order" compared to what you thought it would look like, but that doesn't make it wrong or slow or "off." It just means you have to adjust and have faith that your big moments are still on their way.

Get it out in the open.

It's ok to talk about yucky feelings to your friend when she's celebrating. Maybe not simultaneously, that could be awkward. But you can be honest about your disappointments in your own life. That's what friends are for. However, it's not ok to blame her for any of your sad feelings. It's not ok to shame her for sharing her news. And it's definitely not ok to end a friendship over it.

But it is ok to be honest. Your friend loves you. She's sharing fun news with you because she wants you to be a part of it. And she doesn't want to hurt you in the process. You, on the other hand, don't want your friend to restrain herself in her moment of pure bliss because of your ego. So what do you do? The only way to prevent walking on eggshells around her is to get out in front of it.

Tell her "I'm so happy for you, but I can't help but think about where I am in my life." Remember that you LOVE her, and ideally you should give her permission to beam in her happiness even though it might give you pain. Just don't lie to her. Your friendship was not built on inauthenticity. It was built on trust. So just come out with it! She is going to understand. As long as you make sure to point out that it isn't HER you are upset with—it's your life circumstances—she is going to try her hardest to understand that perspective and console you when needed.

Always remember, this friendship is about BOTH of you.

It's not ALL about one person and then ALL about another due to circumstances. You have a role in this friendship, and your friend can be there for you just as much as you are there for her. So be honest. Let her help. And together, you two can celebrate your accomplishments and mourn your setbacks together.

Be sure to process it outside of your relationship.

Your friend is more than likely your go-to person for talking things out—and for venting. So once you have come out with the hurt and been honest about your pain, what's next?

It might be overkill to continue to talk about your lack of a boyfriend or crummy job when your friend is just trying to enjoy her moment. You want to be there for each other, but sometimes it's appropriate to find other outlets so things don't get tense.

So, when her happiness highlights your disappointment, it's a good idea to have to find other sources to vent to—**but it can't get back to her.**

Your friend will feel crushed if she knows how much her milestones are truly affecting you, and she may feel hurt that you are going to somebody else to discuss it. So try to keep the venting out of the same social circle. She obviously already knows you are struggling (see above), but she doesn't have to be reminded of it every time she talks to you or a mutual friend. So instead, talk to someone else.

Yes, I am biased, but I personally think it is better for you to talk to a professional because they know how to help you process feelings of jealousy, guilt, shame, and embarrassment. Venting only gets you so far. Use this situation to motivate you to seek out some help. It seriously CANNOT hurt.

If you already have your Caroline, don't let your insecurities get the best of you. Try your hardest to push through and find your inner confidence. Be brave enough to talk about it and make things work out. Because you've got to hold onto her for dear life, even when life pulls you two apart like it did for us.

Yes, there is one not-so-awesome aspect of my fabulous

friendship. And that is the fact that Caroline lives in San Antonio, Texas, and I live in Los Angeles, California.

In fact, Caroline and I haven't lived in the same city in seven years.

And, because we are not childhood friends, we only lived in the same city for four years. Meaning we have been separated for longer than we were ever together.

It really sucks. Like, really sucks. I miss her all the time and wish I had a buddy to roll around town with on a Friday night. And by that, I mean I wish I had someone to order delivery and watch *The Office* reruns with. Let's just say our rocking Friday nights in college typically consisted of overflowing Slurpees and Elle Woods getting a grip on life.

But not sharing those moments anymore doesn't mean our friendship has to end. In fact, if our friendship ended I would be seriously screwed. So instead we employ some long distance friend tactics.

We text regularly, we tag each other in stupid Instagram memes like it's our job, we visit each other when we can, and we always keep each other in the loop. I was there for her surprise engagement; she was there for mine. We make it work. We treat our friendship like you would treat any other relationship—give it time, attention, effort, and respect.

There is a chance you and your Caroline will separate at some point in your lives. Do not let distance be an excuse to grow apart. It might seem easy to let it fall to the wayside because it's not giving you the same benefits as it was before, but don't let distance fool you. It's not as powerful as you think.

If you absorbed anything from this chapter, I truly hope it's that you should hold onto friendships that make you a better person and let go of friendships that don't. Your heart will be so grateful for it. And so will I.

Part 4

Handling your Relationship Status

When looking for a life partner, my advice to women is date all of them: the bad boys, the cool boys, the commitment-phobic boys, the crazy boys. But do not marry them. The things that make the bad boys sexy do not make them good husbands. When it comes time to settle down, find someone who wants an equal partner. Someone who thinks women should be smart, opinionated and ambitious. Someone who values fairness and expects or, even better, wants to do his share in the home. These men exist and, trust me, over time, nothing is sexier.

—Sheryl Sandberg

Do not bring people in your life who weigh you down. And trust your instincts...good relationships feel good. They feel right. They don't hurt. They're not painful. That's not just with somebody you want to marry, but it's with the friends that you choose. It's with the people you surround yourselves with.

—Michelle Obama

10

Unhealthy Relationships

If you are in a relationship AND simultaneously fighting off a quarter-life crisis, God bless you.
Whether you are in the most amazing relationship of your life or your love is hanging on by a thread, it should be easy to acknowledge that your relationship has an immense amount of influence over your happiness. Sharing your life with someone involves sharing their ups and downs as well as yours—and that's a lot of emotional pressure if one or both of you are having a tough time transitioning into full-blown adulthood.

Of course, your relationship might be the one beacon of light in your life right now, and that's amazing. But you can't ignore that this phase is still putting a lot of pressure on your relationship. So ideally this section will help you identify some pressure points and give you some insight into what you need to focus on in order to continue to nurture your relationship during this rough patch.

However, if you have some suspicions that your current relationship is *the* source—or, at least a source—of anxiety, then please, please, please do not skip over this.

It's no surprise at this point thanks to the opening quotation that I believe Sheryl Sandberg has some of the best relationship advice out there. As well as her advice to play the field without committing, Sandberg believes that the biggest career choice you will ever make in your life is choosing who to marry. I. Love. It.

And I think it goes even deeper with that. I truly believe that being in a relationship with the wrong person can affect every facet of your life in more ways than you could possibly imagine. It can affect your mood, your self-confidence, your resilience, your self-talk, your career decisions, your inspiration, your motivation, your patience, your tolerance, and your optimism.

The wrong or right partner can influence everything.

I met my now fiancé, Andrew, just as I was coming out of my dreadful quarter-life crisis—and I know for a fact that wasn't a coincidence. I had been working for years to reinvent myself. Years. And it turns out, the final push I needed came from someone else.

I know he isn't the soul reason I finally felt at peace again, but there is no doubt he was a major positive influence on my life when I needed it most. He mirrored back to me what I had been trying to prove to myself from the start: that I was worthy of a confident, creative, and positive life. Maybe I didn't need that reassurance. Maybe I would have found it by myself. But I'm so thankful and happy that it did come from him because I'm a much happier person for it.

Our relationship isn't perfect—by no means—but it is healthy. I can safely say that. We balance each other out in ways I didn't even know I needed. We challenge each other to reach one level higher than what we thought was possible. We defend each other always—no matter how crazy it feels. It can be exhausting at times. It's not easy dating someone more intelligent and more patient than yourself. However, I know that I am growing every day thanks to his character.

But what if Andrew had been a shit head? What if our relationship was textbook terrible? Can you imagine how that could have influenced my precarious confidence?

It's like I was the groundhog coming out of my burrow for the first time in months. Had I seen my shadow in the form of an attractive asshole, I would have retreated back into my old habits and stayed sad for only God knows how much longer. Instead, I chose Andrew and made the decision to continue on as I was. *Hopeful.*

Let me tell you, I could have easily chosen an attractive asshole. They are *everywhere.* Their standards are nonexistent but their charm game is strong. You meet them once and before you know it, you are tangled in an unhealthy relationship without a clear vision of how you even got there in the first place. It used to be my specialty. But I decided to change my habits because dating the right person is not about luck or about fate. It's about smart decision-making.

Unhealthy relationships have the capacity to undo all of the hard work we have done in a matter of weeks. They are a threat to our idealism and the faith we have in our future. They scare the shit out of me, and they should scare the shit out of you, too.

So let's talk about what an unhealthy relationship and a healthy relationship look like.

First of all, let's get one thing straight: unhealthy relationships, *generally*, do not happen overnight. They are a slow burn—like a tiptoe into the water kind of thing. Some of us probably aren't even aware of the dangerous direction our precious relationship is slipping into—and but a lot of us simply turn a blind eye. The real issue? **Once the bleeding starts, it is infinitely difficult to reverse the damage.**

So here is the deal: if you recognize ANY of these symptoms in your relationship, you both need to make a commitment to make some very large changes. You cannot tackle an unhealthy relationship AND a quarter-life crisis at the same time. And why would you want to? You deserve more. So please make the promise to have an open conversation wit your partner. Otherwise, you need to get out. Soon.

Enmeshment

This is the start of it all—the smoking gun. The reality is, at some point in our lives, we are all guilty of this.

Enmeshment is a concept introduced by Salvador Minuchin to describe relationships with loose boundaries, little separateness, and a hyper-concern for others in the relationship that leads to diminished self-autonomy.

For reference, a boundary is a line between where your responsibility ends and another's begins. They are also defined as limits you set between you and others to keep out thoughts, activities and other things that are not in your best interest.

The scariest part about enmeshment is that it feels comfortable. It mimics intimacy with the person you love. You might think you are in a healthy relationship because you feel so close with your partner, but in reality, you two are overlapping each other instead of complementing each other. Closeness is lovely—but needing constant intense interactions is not so lovely. Essentially, we use the other person for safety, self-worth, well-being and security.

Here is where it gets really tricky: When a change occurs in one person, it creates a reverberation across the entire "system" (aka, our relationship). We get lost in the relationship, and our identity is no longer our own. Essentially, our boundaries are so weak that functioning as an individual becomes difficult.

Here's a common example: You had an amazing day—your boss complimented your hard work, you had a bomb ass lunch and you hit all green lights on the way home. Boom. However, your significant other had a shit day—their tire blew out, they bombed a presentation and they stained their favorite shirt. You both arrive home and start chatting about your days. All of a sudden, your mood starts to decrease. You become upset and sad. But wait a minute—these feelings are not representative of your day, but rather your partner's day. Now your day has completely shifted in the opposite direction.

We often mistake the shift in our emotions and mood as empathy. THIS. IS. WRONG. Instead, **you are allowing another person's reality become your own.** Instead of standing at the top of the ditch extending an arm to help them out, you have jumped into the ditch with them. Now you're both stuck.

You can only imagine how complicated this can become when you are trying to navigate your own quarter-life crisis. You are handling enough on your own, but now you are being sucked into your partner's issues as well. You are not only processing your own emotions but now you are processing your partner's, as well. And that is way too much for one person to handle.

A healthy relationship comprises of being there for each

other and problem solving with each other while recognizing that your emotions are yours alone. You are allowed to experience your own emotions without infringing on your partner's, and you can still be there as a source of solace and support for them when they are feeling down. You both are still in it together, but there is a healthy about of separateness that keeps you both autonomous. Remember that you can share your space, finances, or food all you want—but always keep your emotions separate.

Co-dependency

Enmeshment, if fostered long enough, evolves into co-dependency. Essentially, you have morphed from a full individual into someone who actively needs someone else to feel complete. Not only can this deteriorate your confidence, self-esteem, self-worth, and autonomy, but it can also turn you into a completely different person.

Let's continue on with the first example stated above:

Let's say you are the partner who had a totally shit day. You come home, and dang, your partner isn't home because they're working late on a big project. But that doesn't just mean that you have a few hours to yourself, it means that you are physically incapable of self-soothing and recovering from your day by yourself. You have become so dependent on your partner that the idea of cheering up alone seems impossible.

So you sit alone, stew, and become even more upset. What could have been a few hours to reboot before your partner comes home has now become a pressure cooker of misery.

Co-dependency can end up creating a power dynamic

within the relationship that can become dangerous. You are now extremely susceptible to a controlling and manipulative partner who can use their influence to encourage harmful and unhealthy behaviors.

A healthy relationship involves leaning into our partners, not to relying on them. Healthy relationships treat partners as a BONUS, not a necessity. We need to be meeting needs for ourselves and allowing other people to tag along for the ride.

Ways to combat against co-dependency are leaning back into your own coping skills and creating some healthy space between you and your partner. The more you rely on yourself, the less susceptible you will be to having a co-dependent relationship.

Collusion

All right, girls. At this point, we have officially fallen down the rabbit hole.

Once enmeshment creeps into co-dependency, co-dependency then turns into the ugly monster we tend to think we will never fall victim to—**abuse**.

Abuse, generally, starts with some kind of power shift. The ability to make all the decisions: financial choices, friendships we do or do not entertain, places we go, clothing we wear, etc. This abuse of power creates an unhealthy, boundary violating relationship. Remember—abuse is not always physical. When we stop making decisions for ourselves that benefit our well being, abuse can become mental, verbal, emotional or sexual.

As much as I like to joke about pretty much anything, this is never funny. In fact, it's really fucking serious.

If you feel controlled, trapped, manipulated, or stifled, these are all warning signs that this relationship is not healthy. Every relationship has its ups and downs, but feeling powerless is not normal. Ever. So be sure to ask yourself a few questions to make sure you feel safe and secure in your current relationship:

"Do I feel free to make decisions for myself?"

"Do I feel safe asking for what I want?"

"Am I allowed to create a safe space for myself?"

"Do I feel like I'm walking on eggshells around my partner?"

If you answered "no" to the first three or "yes" to the fourth, please acknowledge that your relationship is not safe space for your own personal development. It is in your best interest to leave as soon as you possibly can so your healing can begin.

I'll admit, sometimes it's not as easy as unhealthy vs. healthy relationships. You might be thinking "my relationship MIGHT be unhealthy, but we don't quite fall into that description." That might be true, but don't dismiss the fact that your relationship still might not be healthy, especially if it's brand new.

Dating someone in the very beginning is always fun. There's kissing and cuddling and secret sharing and learning and bonding and more kissing. It's just enough to distract you from your looming quarter-life crisis and get you out of your funk. And thank God for that. In fact, you're so grateful and excited you can't even see straight!

And that's the problem.

Jumping into a new relationship out of pure distraction can cause you to miss a lot of red flags that are lurking around. Instead of looking out for those bright indicators that things aren't what we think they are, we view the world with rose-colored lenses and let anything suspicious pass us by. But red flags are NOT for decoration. There are always signs that a relationship isn't really what it's cracked up to be.

I don't necessarily want you to feel like you have to turn into a detective every time you start dating someone new, but I do want you to be aware. Right now you are more vulnerable than ever to jumping into something that simply isn't right for you, so I want you to watch out for these basic warning signs.

1. He builds desire for himself.

These guys use the basic principles of economics—supply and demand— to ensure that they are always needed. It's utterly and completely manipulative, but it can also be difficult to detect. And at some point or another, it's probably fooled all of us (guilty).

It's simple, really. They believe there is only one of them running around (the supply), so they create an insane amount of demand to make it seem like they are one hot commodity. They restrict time, affection, love, or dates in order to get you to see that they are in hot pursuit by everyone else, including you. Ideally, we would wake up and realize that while he might have special qualities, we aren't hard up for finding acceptable dates. But usually, we get sucked in—because it's so easy to want what you can't have.

The most blatant display of this behavior is when they openly flirt or text other girls while you two are dating to get you to see that he is SUPER DESIRABLE. Gah, he's just the best.

So why do they do this? Well, they are trying to show you that they are someone worth fighting/waiting/pining for. They are trying to be the Millennial's version of Ty Beanie Babies.

What they aren't realizing is that this behavior is also a major sign of low self-esteem. Deep down they believe that the only reason someone of your stature would date someone like them is only through manipulation and circumstance. It's really sad, too, because other than their low self-esteem they might actually be a pretty decent guy. Unfortunately, they can't be bothered to do the self-work to correct it.

It's worth noting that you do not have to stoop to this level. Those of us with higher self-esteem attract others by being a nice human being, not by dangling our goodies in front of somebody else and then taking them away for fun.

The difficult part is catching this behavior while you are already "in" it. It's tough to see the full gravity of what's happening. So try to remember that this quest for attention, compliments, and love **will never end.** Not because you aren't fabulous, but because his thirst for love will only be quenched via self-work and self-acceptance. And that is not your job. That isn't even my job. That's *his* job.

So please, please, please, the next time you see the ole supply and demand trick in full swing, sell your stocks and get the hell out.

2. He's self-centered.

When he asks you a question, is he really wanting to know the answer? Or is he simply waiting for his turn? If you hesitated for ONE second, you're toast.

Self-centered guys can't help but put their own happiness first. And you know, it's totally fine if his happiness is really important to him. But yours should be, too. These are the guys who assume that whatever constitutes a rocking Thursday night for them, will also mean you are on Cloud 9, too. Does he think about what you like to do? Who you like to see? What makes you feel excited? Or is it all cigars, golf, cigars, hunting, beer...and more cigars?

Your clothes are going to reek.

It's normal for there to be compromise in relationships, but it's not normal for one mentality to rule the entire dynamic. Make sure there is a give and take, or else you might be dating someone who has their head shoved so far up his butt, that he doesn't even remember you're there.

3. He doesn't invite you out.

The second a guy kisses a girl for the first time, he can no longer use the 'girls have cooties' bit to justify never wanting to actually hang around girls. He finally has to admit that girls are awesome. Because we really freaking are.

Yes, I am aware that guys need their bromances just as much as we need our precious girl time. But let us ask you this: the last time you saw a group of guys in their 20s hanging out, what happened?

Let us guess. They came over and approached girls to hang. Right? Right. Because girls don't have cooties. Girls have much better things. And guys want to be around girls.

We have finally reached the age of maturity where it's totally normal for the opposite sexes to want to hang out together. We actually enjoy each other's company and respect each other's opinions!

...which is why it's WEIRD that your pseudo-boyfriend is not asking you to hang out with him and his friends.

In fact, Andrew likes to tell people that I'm his little Chihuahua. Not because I yap a lot, but because he likes to takes me everywhere. I'm a good time.

You bring something to the table, too. I shouldn't even have to say that. You are a fun person and you play well with others. Even if you don't want to go to every event your boyfriend wishes to attend, an invite is probably acceptable, right? You want him to meet and hang with your friends, he wants you to meet and hang with his friends. So yes, if he's not inviting you out with him to weddings, birthday parties, special events, or for a random outing of Top Golf...that's a red flag. Bro time isn't that awesome. He can make room for you, too.

4. He shames you.

So let's say he's done a few dumb things, but if you really think about it, you could rationalize most of them. But then...something happens that you can't quite get your mind around. It's the straw that breaks the camel's back. So you scrape up the courage to talk to him about it. You explain your feelings as calmly as you possibly can, and hope for the best.

And then he shames you for it.

This is also called gaslighting. He makes you feel crazy for having any emotion whatsoever.

I don't care what person, what setting, or what circumstance that causes you to bring up your feelings in an appropriate manner—they will ALWAYS deserve to be heard. You ALWAYS have the right feel understood, especially by a significant other. He doesn't have to agree, but he should at least try.

Sure, you might want to work on your delivery (it is ALL in the delivery), but you should at least be able to explain how you feel without feeling stupid for it. In fact, you should be proud of yourself for having the guts, to be honest. And shame on him for making you second-guess it! Feelings are not crazy, feelings are just feelings.

Personal foul on the play. (I'm so punny!)

5. He's sexist.

You know this guy. I know this guy. We all know this guy. Hopefully, though, you aren't dating this guy. Because fuck this guy.

He's the one who talks to you in that condescending tone whenever you do anything wrong. You know, the sexist tone, that subliminally says, "poor stupid girl, you just don't know any better!" He pats you on the head when you try to stick up for yourself. He casually mentions that "women aren't cut out for things"—even when that might be your chosen profession. He calls your friends "crazy" and still believes women aren't funny.

Gawd my hands are shaking in anger just writing this. I HATE THIS GUY. I mean God, his misogyny is so blinding it's a scientific miracle that we are able to stand close enough for him to stare at our breasts all day. In his eyes, you are not his equal. And unless you grow a penis overnight, this dynamic won't change.

It can be surprisingly challenging to detect these guys because a lot of us give them the "macho guy" pass. We say, "He's a guy's guy" or "He's just super masculine, that's all." Because we want someone with hair on their chest. Someone who can fix things around the house. Someone who isn't afraid of spiders.

I get it. I really do. Those can be attractive qualities to a lot of us, and there's nothing wrong with that. But nothing about being a guy's guy has literally anything to do with being a sexist butthead.

You are absolutely allowed to date the star quarterback or the burly hunter, as long as he respects you as a HUMAN BEING and treats you well. If you detect an inch of sexism or condescension, please don't waste any more of your time. A man can be a feminist and macho at the same time. The two are not mutually exclusive.

Lastly, I want to talk about bad habits that can turn into a good relationship into an unhealthy relationship VERY quickly. These following behaviors can be hard to break, yes, but don't freak—these behaviors do not have to be permanent. A lot of us partake in these nasty behaviors without even realizing it, but with some awareness and determination, you can kick them for good.

Do not mind read.

Unless you're a bona fide psychic, you cannot mind read. And neither can they. So don't a) try it, or b) expect it. Communication is what keeps relationships healthy, strong, and LONG. Your partner cannot read your mind, and therefore you will have to thoroughly explain things to them on a daily basis. Things like how you feel, things you expect, what you hope for, and how you would like things to be done. Because they don't know. They only know when you tell them. And then they know.

And same for you! You can't assume you know everything about your partner. People aren't static. We shift from moods and states of emotion and we change opinions all the time.

Or at least I do. So use your language skills and quit reading minds. It will eliminate way more fights, and make it all crystal clear.

Do not play Hot Potato with your feelings. "You're making me feel like this!"

No no no no no.

You can't throw your feelings at someone else and make them take responsibility. That's not how this goes. You feel a certain way because that's how you feel. Your feelings are not debatable. They aren't facts that you can rip apart and analyze from different angles. They're feelings. And the only one who can label them, share them, or explain them, is you.

So...that means your partner can't take responsibility. Instead, you can inform them why you feel a certain way. Something like...

"I feel CRAPPY when you say CRAPPY THINGS."

Well, maybe not exactly like that. But you get the point. Take responsibility for your emotions and communicate them as calmly as you can.

Do not aim to win.

If you win a fight, then the relationship loses. And believe us, noooooooobody wins if the relationship doesn't win.

When a fight occurs, and you come out with guns blazing, ready to explain why you are completely right and he is absolutely wrong, check yourself. And do it quickly.

Really, what are you going to gain from this? Credibility? If that? And why would you even need that, if the person you are trying to prove yourself to, is the one person you don't have to prove yourself to?

Put the swords down, and work together to make sure you both end up on common ground. Talk it out. Yes, you can absolutely explain yourself, but they get that chance, too. You two have got to make sure that you both feel heard and validated, and that way, the relationship can shine through.

I know being a loser sucks. But this is the one case where being a loser could actually save your relationship.

Do not bottle up feelings.

Awful awful awful awful bad bad bad bad.

You know how it starts. Something bothers you, but you don't want to be 'that girl,' so you let it slide. And then something else happens, but you can't really say anything, because you didn't say anything about the first thing, so they didn't really know how you were feeling anyway. Ugh. So you tuck it away. Then a few more little things happen, but they're too small to really even mention, so those get tossed to the side, too.

And then it happens. They don't turn the air conditioning off before you leave the house. (Hello, electric bill.) They say a sarcastic comment that could easily be seen as humor…but it's not really funny. Rude. They forget to do that favor they promised you, because, well, they were super busy.

GOODBYE, SANITY. Feelings start gushing out of you. They can't stop! They WON'T stop! OH MY WORD I CANNOT FIGURE OUT HOW TO CAP THIS EMOTIONAL WELL.

Well…you can't. Not now. Not until every feeling is completely out in the open and nothing else is bottled up. And now you have a big fat fight on our hands and everything is messy and ew.

Don't bottle up your feelings. Nags are called nags because they aren't nice about communicating their feelings—not because they share them. Don't be afraid to let people know how you feel in a kind fashion. You're a nice person. You don't want to complain all the time. But you also can't be a doormat.

So share your feelings and spare yourself and your relationship an emotional meltdown every other month!

11

Ending a Relationship

So have I thoroughly scared the bejeezus out of you yet? I'm truly sorry if I am being blunt and causing you to question your semi-decent relationship. Kind of. Ok fine, you caught me. I'm not sorry. At all.

I think you are deserving of a great relationship because you aren't afraid to do some major self-development yourself. Shouldn't you have a mate who will do the same? Leaving a decent relationship might just be the one thing standing in your way of an amazing relationship.

I'll be the first to admit that relationships have rough patches all the time. In fact, I call them "growing pains." Many relationships hit tumultuous times when two big personalities are adjusting to one another. It's normal. So, trust me when I say: not every rough patch means the relationship should be over.

Alas, the question remains: *When is it actually time to end a relationship?* When is a rough patch no longer a rough patch, but a pattern?

Here is how you know when it's time to end a relationship:

You don't like yourself in the relationship.

You know how colors look differently when lined up next to each other? Your blue eyes POP when you're wearing navy, hunter green, or purple—but they glaze over when wearing white or gray. The same happens with people.

People can complement our personalities in vastly different ways. Some can bring out your inner stand-up comedian, while others encourage your intellectual, professorial side to really blossom under pressure. It's not crazy to say that your romantic partner has the most influence over this complementary dynamic—so be honest with yourself when you ask—do you like yourself in this relationship?

Are you loving this confident, kind, ambitious, and empathetic you, or are you consistently coming face to face with your icky side?

We all have flaws. We all have demons. It's not that we want to completely erase them—but we don't want to highlight them, either. And if our partner consistently brings out the worst in us, it's going to be hard to thoroughly enjoy the relationship.

I want to make one thing exceptionally clear: this isn't necessarily your partner's fault.

Your partner most likely cannot help how their personality complements yours. But regardless—you deserve to be in a relationship where you feel like a better person for it.

There isn't perceived equity in effort.

Do you feel like you're carrying the relationship? Are you the one always reaching out? Making plans? Showing affection? Sharing stories?

Oof. You must be exhausted.

People share and receive love in different ways. Your relationship does not need to be quid pro quo down the line. But if you don't perceive the relationship as being equal—that is a massive problem.

Everyone is busy. Everyone has baggage. Everyone has obligations. But when you're in a relationship, you make time for it, period. Otherwise, you guys can just date and casually enjoy each other's company while you keep on living your life. Relationships require effort and commitment. So if you're not perceiving either—then what's the point? You deserve to be courted just as much as you should be expected to do the courting. Walking away at least gives you the opportunity to find a balanced relationship.

You don't feel loved.

One of the best perks of being in a relationship is having the solid belief that you are *special.* They chose YOU. You get their kisses. You get their compliments. You get their affection. You are the one who gets to be their partner, and they get to be yours. You are the queen of the relationship kingdom.

So if you don't feel this way, *again*, what's the point?

Not feeling loved has got to be one of the worst feelings EVER. Yes, I am all for self-love and completely encourage women to love themselves so much that it doesn't matter what other people think. But subjecting ourselves to feeling not loved on a daily basis just sounds like misery stew.

That's a hard pass from me. And it should be for you, too.

The reality is, life is hard. There are going to be moments in life where you don't feel intelligent. You are going to have days when you think all of your hard work has been pointless. There will be months when you feel like absolutely nothing is going your way. I promise you, it will happen. So in those moments, the last thing you want is a partner who doesn't help build you back up. It's hard convincing ourselves of our worth—**we don't need the duty of convincing our partner, too.**

Let them go, and find someone who is dead sure of your fabulousness.

You know you don't love them.

Do not let guilt, fear, shame, or embarrassment keep you in a relationship. Not only are you doing yourself a disservice, but you are completely screwing over your partner, too.

Breakups are hard. People get their feelings hurt. But human beings are resilient. We are wired for survival. Emotional setbacks are difficult—but we bounce back. In fact, we were designed to bounce back. And the hurt that we suffer is *completely* worth it when we are finally able to find someone who treats us the way we deserve. But guess what? You—nor them—will get that opportunity if you hold onto a loveless relationship because you're scared of short-term consequences.

I say this with love: **get over it.**

You are going to hurt people, and people are going to hurt you. That's life. So do what you know to be right and cut people free when you can't give them what they need. And hope to goodness that they do the same for you.

You love them, but you don't like them.

There is a *massive* difference between like and love. You love your family—but you don't always like your family. You like your next-door neighbor, but you don't love them (especially when their damn dog barks all day). (This is not a personal reference). (Ok, yes it definitely is).

So ask yourself, do you *like* your partner? Do you admire their accomplishments? Do you think they are a good person? Do you like their friends? Are they nice to strangers? Do they tip their waitresses? Do you brag about them to your family?

If you are struggling to come up with concrete things that you like about your partner, that's not a good sign. You need to love AND like your partner. Life is too long to be with someone you tolerate. They can have a good heart, and still not be the one for you. Give yourself permission to find someone who lights your haystack on fire AND is nice to your mother. They're out there. But you won't find them unless you end it.

TL;DR: Relationship Goals: Ben and Leslie from *Parks and Rec*.

You are putting your life on pause.

I'm going to continue repeating this until I am blue in the face: relationships are bonuses in life. The goal is to have an independently happy life, find someone who also has an independently happy life, and share your fabulously independent lives together. So if your life is being put on hold completely because of their choices—that ain't good.

It's ok if there is a little give and take. Your relationship responsibilities won't always be evenly distributed. But you should always be able to pursue your goals, keep moving forward, and build the life you envisioned while you are dating somebody else. The two are not even close to being mutually exclusive.

Andrew and I are actually a fabulous example of this. About a year and a half into our relationship, Andrew decided to settle into early retirement from the law profession. I didn't blame him. Being a lawyer sucks wind.

But before that turning point, I had been planning *my* next career moves. I had gotten a job in private practice, been fired from said job. I had pitched an online coaching platform to a VP of a big time restaurant, been turned down for said pitch, and started building the beginnings of a company I had recently named Blush.

Needless to say, I was doing a lot of the leaning. A lot. My funds were short, my stress was high, and my direction was all over the place. He was my anchor in my messy life.

Was that fair? I don't know. Maybe not. But either way, the tables were quickly turned the second he quit his job. I was now the breadwinner, the anchor, and the homemaker. It was my turn to hold down the fort while he got his life in order. We took turns. And to this day, we still do.

Not every relationship needs to have this dramatic of twists and turns—it can be way more subtle than this. But the point is, you have to have some sort of a balancing act within your relationship. There should not be a pattern of one person taking it all while the other accommodates every step of the way.

In fact, maybe there's a better way of phrasing this: **your significant other is holding you back.**

You can love someone with all your heart, but they just might not be on your same frequency. This might not be their fault. It might not be anyone's fault. But if you can't ignore the reality that your life isn't progressing the way it should because of this relationship—things aren't going to get any better the longer you wait. You're only going to fall further and further behind on your goals, and in the end, you will resent your partner for the lost time. Don't do that to them. Don't do that to yourself. End the relationship and keep moving forward.

The negative outweighs the positive.

This is pretty self-explanatory. If the fighting outweighs the kissing, the crying overshadows the laughing, the knots outweigh the butterflies—then it's time to move on.

Most relationships aren't meant to last. They are meant to teach you something, offer you some amazing memories, and fade away. Give the relationship the dignity it deserves and put it out of its misery. It's dying out, and it deserves a proper burial instead of a slow starvation.

Yes, it's hard. But you're going to be just fine. **So let's talk about getting over a breakup.**

Whether you are currently going through a breakup not by choice, or this book might have made you rethink your current relationship and you are planning for a not-so-fun breakup in the near future, here are some of my best tips for recovery.

It's worth noting that regardless of the nature of the breakup, they hurt like a bitch. This mostly stems from the lack of protection we shield ourselves with during the relationship. Had we known that this relationship was going to rip apart at the seams, we might have held back a little more. But we didn't. So everything hurts. Even our fingernails.

I don't want you to learn how to restrain yourself in relationships. That leads to broken intimacy, minimal communication, insecurity, and whack defense mechanisms. It's not good. But I do want to help you bounce back from heartache. I want you to feel like you can go full throttle into everything relationship you have, and recover just fine if it doesn't work out.

So bear in mind that the good news is **we are resilient.** And instead of learning how to hold back within our relationships, we just have to learn how to get better at overcoming the breakups.

1. Cry.

A lot. Because if you don't do it now—you'll just do it later. And by then, it'll seem a little odd that you're not over it. So go ahead girl—let it out now. Cry in your room, cry in your car, cry to a friend, cry to your mom. Cry until your tear ducts have to work overtime just to supply enough tears to keep you going. Get it ALL out. You have to seriously shed all of this pent up sadness out of your body—or else it will hang around you for weeks to come.

There is absolutely no shame in crying—remember that you weren't prepared for this kind of heartache. You left your heart completely exposed to rejection, and it hurts. Like hell. So honor the gnarly feeling that it is, get back in that shower, and cry like you mean it.

2. Take some space.

As hard as it may be, it's what you need to do. Do not answer that text from him that starts with "Just wanting to check in…" No coffee dates to scream at each other over the loose ends.

And under no circumstances will you engage in the whole "exchanging of the things" to tug on your already shredded heartstrings. If he really needs his dang high school football jersey back then just drop it off at his front door. It's not like anybody is going to steal it—it's gross.

So why am I being so intense about this? Well first, keeping in contact with your ex after a gut-wrenching breakup is delaying your recovery. It erases any progress you've made on your own—because one quick conversation with them reminds you how happy you were pre-split. And all of a sudden, we're back to the uncontrollable crying. Damn it.

Talking also encourages that glimmering shred of hope that you two are getting back together. And that hope is essentially a bungee cord attached to your heart—the second you think you're free of the agony, it snaps you right back in again.

For right now, it's best to do your healing on your own. You are resilient, and you do not need your ex to push you through this. Sure, after you've recovered and healed, being friends with an ex can actually work out sometimes. But until then, take the space to get comfortable in your new life without them.

3. Spend time alone.

You can rebound later. For right now, let's focus on dating yourself.

Don't worry, you're not feeling sorry for yourself if you stay in on a Friday night and binge watch Parks and Rec. (Might I suggest the "Galentine's Day" episode?). Instead, you're simply getting comfortable with being alone. You really haven't had that chance in quite some time. It's fun to reconnect with yourself! You can be the most selfish brat in the world and no one is there to pitch a fit! You can watch your quirky indie comedies, eat frozen yogurt by the gallon, and experiment with creepy skin masks at your leisure. It's quite lovely.

But more than just getting to have it your way—you are overcoming the pervasive fear of being alone. Because if you are scared of being alone, how will you ever know if your next relationship is fueled by love or fear?

Let's make sure we know the answer to that one.

4. Trust fall.

Metaphorically, of course.

It's time to call your friends and family to ask for some super-sized support. Trust me, you do not want to go through a breakup all by yourself. I mean you're already not talking to your ex and spending way more time alone (riiiiight?)—so let's make sure we get some balance up in this joint. Talk, call, text, email, Snapchat, DM, G-chat, and get some FaceTime in there, too. Just make sure you are communicating to your group on a regular basis. Let them know that you're hurting and that you need some backup for the next few weeks (or months—no judgment).

More than being there to give you advice, your support system can be there to distract you and infuse some fun back into your life. So take advantage, and go have fun.

5. Write it out.

You've got a lot going on in your head right now. Questions and cuss words and hypothetical scenarios that will probably never happen keep playing over and over again. It's overwhelming. And it's time to address it. So let's write it out.

Actually, better yet, write it out to the ex.

Yes—write a letter to your ex. Write out how you feel, what you're thinking, how you've been, and any questions you may be trying to figure out. Don't worry, I'm not going to make you send it (that would violate rule #2). This letter is just for you.

This is your time to release everything you've been carrying around and put it all down in one place. And when you're done, you can put it away. Burn it for all I care. Just don't re-read it every night or even think about hitting "send"—it's in the past now. And hopefully, some of those uncomfortable feelings you've been carrying around can stay there, too.

6. Talk it out.

ok, you've got your crew assembled. Your extra positive breakup squad! They'll drop whatever they're doing because they know exactly what you are going through, right?

Good. Now comes the fun part. It's time to thoroughly dive into what in the hell happened that made this break up so freaking awful. And you're going to need a partner in crime to help you work it out.

If you trust one of your besties to hold your hand as you walk through the emotional train wreck that is your heartache, that's seriously amazing. Go for it. But if you're not sure about involving a friend, you might be better off with someone who has experience with this. And sometimes, there's nothing better than a little life coaching or therapy to give you a massive emotional makeover.

The important piece is that you address the dissolution of

the relationship and the aftermath because that's how patterns start to form. You know how one of your friends always dates the same kind of people and ends up in the same situation over and over again? Yeah, you don't want that. And you definitely don't want to coast forward for a few months, trick yourself into thinking you're fine, and then break down after a subpar romantic drama that wasn't even a tearjerker.

This is the time to do the work. Talk it out. Get sad. Get angry. Reflect. Then take a break and come back. Too much heavy handedness will burn you out—but you cannot ignore the deep feelings you're carrying around. So find a balance between reflection and distraction, and keep moving forward.

7. Remain hopeful.

It's easy to fall into pessimistic tendencies after a breakup.

"I'm never going to meet anyone again."
"My life was all about them—what now?"
"I can't trust anyone."

Listen to me: **do not let an ex take away your light.**

You will meet someone again. You will get your life back. And you will trust again. Why? Because you had all of these qualities before. It's not like this breakup went in and changed your DNA. You're still the same you—it's just your perspective is a bit different. Things will revert back to normal if you just trust the system. Let your body work its way through this break up as long as it needs to. Remember that you get to control the amount of self-awareness you pour into this breakup phase. And the more energy you put into pulling yourself out, the easier it will become.

So I want to circle back to this whole not talking to your ex thing. It's important. Like, really important.

Talking to an ex is the single best way to hold onto your sadness. It will keep you attached to a relationship that died months ago—and you don't have time for that. So you cannot talk to them. Cannot. Do. It.

Yes, I know. This is controversial. Experts across the board are coming out in support of being cordial with exes. *Get over it!* they say. *Be grownups! Ditch the pettiness!*

It's almost as if refraining from speaking to an ex is considered the most immature action you could possibly take. But talking to an ex is a lot like drinking an entire bottle of wine in one sitting. It sounds *amazing* in theory, but it's absolutely destructive in action. And it also leaves you with a massive headache.

But before I dive in, I will give two exceptions to this rule. First, if you two have children together, then it's imperative to remain friendly. Co-parenting and keeping a united front for the sake of the child(ren) is highly encouraged and is most likely the best option for the family.

Second, if BOTH parties are COMPLETELY over the relationship, then being friends is totally acceptable. Why not? Platonic friendships are ze best. But before you assume that this exception applies to you—make sure you can prove this theory. For instance, are both of you dating other people? How long has the relationship been over? When's the last time there was a 'moment' between you two? Be honest! If you can safely say that both of you are completely over the other, then all right. You're free to skip this blog.

For the rest of you...here are the most important reasons why you should not talk to your ex while recovering from a breakup:

1. You maintain the connection.

Breakups are rough. Sometimes they blindside you. Sometimes they hang on for dear life, torturing you until the final straw snaps. Nobody likes them, but for the most part, they are a necessary evil of life. But the pain isn't meant to be permanent—it's meant to be a short-term shock to the heart that we can all recover from. That is...unless you keep chatting it up.

Continuously texting, seeing, or speaking to an ex is holding onto a ghost of the relationship. The relationship is over. It's not there anymore. So maintaining it only invests time and energy into something that didn't work out. Instead, you need to be working on closing the connection and dumping your resources into other outlets.

Eventually when both of you have moved forward from the relationship, then you can give some energy towards the connection again. But chances are, you will have moved on by then, and it won't interest you as much as you thought it would.

2. You erase progress.

If you're recovering from a breakup, chances are you've been trying your hardest to move forward. Maybe you've given back some comfy shirts or shared books as a token of the divide. Perhaps you've tried pretty hard not to reach out, even though

the temptation is killing you. And you've hopefully tri
ing it out with friends or family.

So you probably already know that communication
good idea. **Because that's the second you lose a lot**
progress.

It's so easy. You send a text here, a snap there, and
sudden you are knee-deep into old patterns! You're now
when something funny happens. You're sharing the inn
details of your day. Hell, you're even providing them wit
tional support!

But unfortunately, the relationship ended and that's
purpose anymore. Both of you have to move on, but con
cating keeps you stuck.

Eventually one of both of you will realize that this
isn't healthy. Getting back together isn't happening, an
really isn't a point to all this chatting. So then you have
moving on....again.

Ughhhhhhhh jklfdjklafjklafjl. Sorry, my forehead a
fell on the keyboard out of pure agony.

All that earlier progress. Gone. Just, GONE. Bye
Cheers to completely starting over.

Don't do this to yourself. Give yourself the space an
you need to fully move forward. Once you're in a better
then you can rekindle any kind of platonic friendship
like.

3. It gives false hope.

The relationship ended for a reason. It didn't just r
course—there was a firm, legitimate reason the two
couldn't reach the next level. Breakups don't just happe

d talk-

isn't a

f your

ll of a

texting

ermost

emo-

not its

muni-

attern

there

start

tually

Felipe.

time

place,

you'd

in its

f you

n. It's

---

e short stick and had to deal with the
chance. No. There was a conversa-
ality. And it all stemmed from one or

ommunicate like nothing ever hap-
e of falsehood. You get wrapped up
mories, old feelings. Of course, those
lead one of you on—it's almost impos-

reason for the breakup—there was a
hip. You two obviously had a connec-
it's pretty difficult to erase from mem-
y to forget why the relationship ended
started. Don't leave a trail of bread-
on's den when you KNOW it is almost
ve. Protect yourself! Let yourself regain
om the old relationship before you work
onship. Both of you will benefit in the

ortunities.

u're doing all the talking with your ex,
as much talking with people who are
se other people are the people who you
lationship with…unlike a certain some-
g yourself up to new people or exploring
ou're sinking yourself further into a rela-
burnt to the ground. The emotional
nue to pour into an ex could be poured
would gladly return the love. Don't shut

yourself off from opportunities by burying yourself
relationship and open yourself up to new possibilitie:
tion can be a sweet treat after time spent processing
yourself that break.

Don't let a bad breakup or a bad relationship steal y
I know you are struggling right now, but getting ri d
one who holds you back is only going to lighten your
ready to feel a major transformation coming your
don't' be afraid to go through it alone.

in an old
. Distrac-
. so allow

our glow.
of some-
load. Get
vay—and

12

Building a Healthy Relationship

If you are currently in a relationship that is feeling the heat from your intense quarter-life crisis, I hear you. You need not feel guilty or feel like you are ruining this relationship day by day. Relationships are meant to withstand the most difficult of times in our lives, and this is going to be one of them. You can't feel terrible for wanting to keep your fabulous partner while also needing to concentrate on mending yourself back to adulthood.

But you also have to be good to it. Healthy relationships deserve to be nurtured.

As you already know, I met Andrew at one of my lower points. My severe awareness of how much the last three years had changed me was weighing heavy on my shoulders, and I was truly scared I wasn't ever going to regain my sparkle.

I was in the perfect position for self-sabotage. And there were plenty of times I almost did. Vulnerability and honesty were my two saviors.

A little backstory: Andrew and I actually first met when I was 18. I was a college freshman at the University of Texas at

Austin who got busted for alcohol in my dorm room and my lovely RA forced me to come and paint Student Government signs as punishment. Oops. She was running for vice president, and someone named Andrew was running for president. Nerds.

So there I was, 8 AM on a Saturday morning, painting some dude's name over A-frames that were going to stand all over campus. My hung-over 18-year-old self was none too pleased with this arrangement. But somehow I pushed my bratty attitude aside and actually got involved with Student Government. I even went out for a leadership position! I was getting involved! Meeting smart people! Taking myself VERY seriously!

Andrew, of course, gave the position to someone else. I mean, everyone knows that the best love stories start out with mutual hate. He was just doing his job.

So seven years later, I had forgiven him, and we struck up a "friendship." (Aka Kali awkwardly messaging Andrew about her big move to Austin on Facebook Messenger and making him meet her at a bar downtown by himself.)

Right from the onset, something was weird. We didn't know how to small talk. Within the first five minutes of seeing each other, I launched into how the last few years of my life were super sucky. He figured so much because as he so gracefully put it, I "ghosted" after college. Thanks, babe.

But he hadn't had it easy, either. He told me about his mom passing away and his hatred for his job. He discussed his last relationship and how it ended in the most explosive way you could ever imagine (that's a whole other book) and how he wasn't sure he was reaching his full potential. He was so…disappointed. With life. With everything.

Yeah, I knew a little something about that.

Our collective jadedness left zero room for sugarcoating. We went straight for the real stuff. There were no mixers in our truth-telling—it was like the conversational equivalent of a scotch on the rocks.

Life hadn't turned out the way we expected it to. And being able to talk about it was just...magic. That was how we established the nature of our relationship. From then on out, we were going to do things our way.

For our first date, he asked me to be his plus one on a work trip to the Sundance Film Festival. I was so freaked out I hung up on him the first time he asked, but thanks to a little encouragement from my dad (what a gem), I accepted. Less than 24 hours later we hopped on a plane together and had the most fun either of us had had in a long time.

Four years later, we're still having fun. But it hasn't always been easy.

We both have big personalities and a lot of strong values. Our lack of sugarcoating makes us very susceptible to hurt feelings and foot-in-mouth moments. Our mutual determination to chase careers we love have at different times left us both unemployed, job hunting, making minimum wage, and very stressed out.

But we keep working on our relationship. We know it's worth it. No matter how difficult things get, we continue to work on being respectful, loving, supportive, and caring. And that can be the absolute hardest thing in the world to pull off when you're cranky and hungry and trying your hardest not to turn on the air conditioning because you know your electric bill will be outrageous and monies are tight.

He is much better at keeping it together than I am, so at least I have someone to look up to.

Our relationship is very flawed, and that's ok. It doesn't need to be perfect. And while I may not be the world's best girlfriend, I did manage to help keep this healthy relationship intact during some rough transitions. I think that's worth something. So I want to share with you some of the tips that have helped me over the past four years.

First, let's talk about building trust.

Love is nothing without trust. And I love love. Very much. I think love is the single most incredible feeling in the entire world. But it doesn't have a shot at lasting without trust.

I also value trust because I don't think it comes very easily. Love is impulsive. It's irrational and illogical and uncontrollable. We don't teach ourselves to fall in love. We don't force it, either. It just happens. Anybody can fall in love. But not everybody can trust.

Trust takes work. It takes dedication. It takes maturity. And it takes a lot of self-development. It's the blue ribbon in a sea of participation certificates. So it's no wonder that those of us who haven't reached the pinnacle of trust desperately want to conquer it.

But I will tell you right now—it is WORTH the effort. Having trust as the solid foundation of your relationship makes everything that much easier to overcome together It is what will carry you through the easy times, the hard times, and the in between times.

Here's how you develop trust in your relationship:

1. Let go of all the small things.

Ok, I'll admit it. This is probably the chicken and the egg thingamabob. If you don't trust someone, you probably pick at all of the small things. Or, is it that if you pick at all of the small things, you inherently lose trust? Honestly, who cares. Neither is good.

Small things are the bane of a healthy relationship's existence. There is absolutely no reason to focus your hard earned energy on something insignificant in a relationship. The key, however, is what's supposed to be labeled an insignificant 'small thing,' or an important 'small thing'?

Values. It's all in the values.

If your significant other does something that violates a value of yours—that's not a small thing. And *this* is exactly how the small things compile into one, large, scary monster that explodes all over your pretty relationship. They were NEVER small things. They just didn't get the attention they deserved.

However, for the other small things, the things that might bother you but don't necessarily violate a value of yours—let it go. Trust that your partner has good intentions. Trust that your partner didn't mean a thing by it. Trust that your partner has your back. Trust that your partner slipped up. Whatever it is, trust that you don't have to call out every small thing in order to have a great relationship. Build the trust, and let it go.

2. Focus on the facts.

Trust is all about perception. If we perceive that someone loves us, then we trust that they love us. It's as simple as that. So use all of the facts you perceive to be true in your life to support building trust in your life. It sounds complicated, but it's not.

Here are some common facts about relationships:
1. You are in a monogamous relationship.
2. Your partner is a good person.
3. You mean a great deal to them.
4. They do nice things for you.
5. They like spending time with you.

Those are ALL amazing facts. Now, there might be some other not so amazing facts in your corner as well. Things like…
1. Your partner doesn't always have the right thing to say at the right moment.
2. They have bad days because of work or other life stressors.
3. Sometimes when they get busy, they don't text as often.
4. PDA isn't really their thing.
5. They are bad at planning.

You can choose to focus on the first five facts, or you can choose to focus on the latter five facts. Totally up to you. But one of them is going to build trust, and the other isn't. And I am going to assume that you like this person and want to be in a relationship with this person and think they are deserving of your love—hence, you know, the relationship. So give positivity a shot. The more beneficial factors you perceive, the more trust you will build. Positive facts will always be your greatest relationship asset.

3. Always be honest.

Always. Always. Always.

We've all read/seen *Gone Girl.* We all know "Cool Amy." The girl who drinks regular Coke and eats pizza because it's "cool"—but secretly hates what she's doing to her body. On the surface, she never cares about dirty jokes or sexism, she plays video games and LOVES sports. Nothing bothers her. Ever. In fact, she's so go-with-the-flow you wonder if ANYTHING will push her buttons. She even has a smile on her face when her boyfriend is acting like a total buttface.

Please don't be the "cool girl" because you think you have to be in order to gain the respect of a man. You don't have to drink Budweiser or watch action films or anything else unless YOU want to. Otherwise, it's fake. And that can only last for so long.

Now, I'm not calling you a sociopath if you've ever done this before. WE ALL HAVE. Cool Kali watched Sports Center and loved skiing and shot-gunned beers because, hey, it's Wednesday! Let's just say real Kali can't tell you one player on the LA Lakers, (Is Shaq still there?) hates cold weather more than black olives on pizza, (seriously freaking gross) and pretty much only drinks red wine and rosé. Sipping—not chugging.

If someone met Cool Kali and then turned around to find out that Real Kali is nothing like her...how could there be any trust? And how pissed off would that guy be? (lol)

Anyway, the point is you can't have trust in someone else if you aren't even being honest with yourself. If you are "putting on a show" for someone else—that is a huge red flag. More than likely you feel like you aren't good enough in your natural state, or that your partner is probably faking things for you, too.

Ouch.

This is where the insecurity, suspicious thoughts, and paranoia come from. This is where trust goes to die. And in order to resurrect it, you have to be honest.

When your partner violates one of your values, speak up. If they piss you off, say something. If they do something absolutely incredible and you want to shower them with love, kiss them! Don't hold yourself back. Be unapologetically you. Because if you can be your most vulnerable, your most authentic, and your most uninhibited version of yourself, you will ignite that in your partner as well. And just like that: trust will blossom all over the damn place.

Yay!

4. Set boundaries.

I know we already covered this—but I am going to reiterate for emphasis' sake.

Do not be afraid to set boundaries and stick to them—especially when it comes to trust. Privacy—boundaries in particular—are rather important for trust. We have a tendency to…snoop…if you will, when we feel anxious or unsettled about the security of our relationship. So it's best to think about what is acceptable and what is unacceptable for privacy concerns in relationships.

For example, I've been in relationships where reading each other's text messages, emails, or anything else is an absolute no-no. That is a complete violation of privacy, and if one violates that boundary, there will be consequences that usually come in the form of someone getting bitched out.

Good times.

My current relationship has almost the opposite take on things. Emails, text messages, and the like are free game. It's not a mandatory thing. In fact, it's not really a thing at all. It's just a casual approach towards privacy. Everything is pretty much out in the open. Passwords are shared (but mostly for convenience) and anything goes.

This made a surprise engagement a bit tricky on Andrew's end, so he semi-regretted this policy for a good three months. Comes with the territory.

Neither scenario is wrong (sans the bitching out part). Each relationship has their own rules and that's great as long as it's agreed upon. But it's imperative to dig deep in order to figure out your boundaries. And then you have to share them. This is a collaborative experience—be sure to ask about your partner's boundaries and make a real solid effort to respect them every inch of the way.

5. Relinquish control.

Not as easy as it sounds. But we gotta try.

In order to trust, you have to let go. You have to give your partner enough credit not to micromanage, remind, belittle, or question. You just have to trust that they value you as a friend, as a partner, and as a person.

So you have to trust that they will see cute humans around and not act on anything. You have to trust that they are respecting you no matter how far away they might be at certain times. You have to trust that they always have your back, no matter how high the cards are stacked up against you.

Anything short of this isn't trust. It's conditional. And it's not a way to sustain a relationship.

You can still share control of the relationship with your partner (along with life circumstance), but you cannot control your partner. And in trying to do so, you will only make yourself miserable. Control's side effects show up in nasty panic attacks, self-sabotage, paranoia, insecurity, jealousy, and anger. It's not pretty. And you know what I'm talking about because we have all felt it at some point or another.

Don't do this to yourself. Let go of control. Because the less you try to control, the more you will rely on trust.

If you continue to build trust every day, slowly but surely you'll see that you can start exploring hard topics you thought you would always have to avoid.

Topics like...the Ex Files.

I know. Exes are taboo.

Nobody likes to bring them up. They make us feel insecure, anxious, and sometimes out of our damn minds. I know I already told you not to talk TO your ex, but talking ABOUT them is a totally different story.

I know you aren't going to like this, but I'm going to say it anyway: It's a good thing to talk about your exes in relationships.

Ya. Sounds crazy, right? But in reality, it's not. We already know that healthy relationships are built on trust. They can handle anxiety-provoking topics like finances, intimacy, family dynamics, and much more...so they can handle this, too. So you've gotta do it. You've gotta talk about them.

Not every day, not even every month—but nonetheless, it's important. And I'm going to tell you why.

1. It keeps you sane.

Admit it: when you enter into a new relationship, part of you wonders how they're still single. They're amazing! It's a miracle! Everything is perfect!

But then you realize: there IS a reason they are single. It's most likely because they went through a breakup. Maybe even a recent breakup.

Let the spiraling out of control thoughts commence.

What's she like? Is she cuter than me? Is she smarter than me? Did he like her more than me? Did he break up with her? Did she break up with him? OMG why would she break up with him? He's perfect. I have to find out. What's her last name? I'll find her on social media. DAMN her account is private. Ugh it's ok I'll have Karen follow her. OMG she is skinnier than me. And has better hair. What the &*#$?

No no no no no no no no no.

Instead of jumping to your own conclusions, villainizing a poor girl you don't even know, or doing some irresponsible social media stalking—get the facts from the horse's mouth. This will curb any impulses you might have to fabricate a story of the past that shouldn't have much of anything to do with your future.

Plus, there are lots of other benefits from having this conversation. Continue on, please.

2. It gives you context.

Ok, you're in. You've brought up the Ex Files and you are swimming in dark waters. But don't fear—you are going to learn a lot.

Understanding someone's previous relationships gives you insight into their priorities, values, triggers, and non-negotiables. It gives you an inside peek into what makes this person tick, and what's enough to end a relationship. This conversation doesn't have to change anything about yourself—you might have things in common with an ex, and that's great. It's normal for us to gravitate towards people with similarities. That's why it's called "having a type."

On the flip side, you might have a lot of differing qualities, and that's ok, too. Perhaps your partner went through a big self-discovery phase and learned a lot about himself and you get a front row seat on their evolution.

Same goes for you, by the way. Discussing your previous relationships and your exes does the same for your partner. Yes, it's painful. Yes, there will be some questions you don't want to answer and some questions you don't want to ask. That's ok. Be in tune with your values. Be aware of your boundaries—and feel confident enough to set them out loud when you're feeling too anxious.

3. It normalizes the past.

We all want that dark, looming cloud to go away. The one that holds all of the unknowns about our current partner. We try to ignore it, but no matter how hard we push it away, it's always there. The ONLY way to make it float away, is to discuss it. The elephant in the room is only ushered out once he is recognized.

The good news is, most of the time, a person's exes aren't going to be monsters. Sure, we all have that *one* ex that we would love to never, ever, see again (HEY JOHN)...but otherwise, most of them are pretty decent humans. We all dated them for a reason, right? And just because things didn't work out doesn't mean they turned into horrible people overnight.

Pro Tip: If someone hates every single one of their exes with a fiery passion—chances are the exes aren't the problem. Either they blame all of their issues on others, or they have really bad taste in human beings.

So when talking about exes, try to keep that in mind when listening to the stories. It's so easy to be intimidated by the past. It's foreign. Unknown. Scary. We can assume and complicate and bend and project onto it all day long. But actually discussing it and taking away the mystery of it all only loosens up the tension surrounding it.

Once you talk about your previous relationships, they aren't taboo anymore. They feel like normal stories that everybody has. It doesn't give you that pit in your stomach anymore. It's not interesting. It's just the past. The boring, silly, old past that will remain behind you as you continue building your future together.

4. It aligns you together.

When you're feeling insecure about your partner's ex, it's easy to subconsciously form teams. Team Ex and Partner VS. You. You feel alone. Attacked. Annoyed. Angry. And lots of other A words.

You start to convince yourself that the ex and your partner have more of an affiliation than they do with you. It's a reasonably new relationship after all, and they used to date for a while. I get that it's easy to start thinking like that. But this is why talking about it is so important.

Once you begin a dialogue about previous relationships, you

realign your teams. Now you're "in" on the skinny! You know details, too. You get what happened. You have the inside scoop. So now it's You and Partner VS Ex.

You two together against the world! No ex-relationship is going to get in your way. You two have it handled! Teammates fo' life!

5. It opens the door for more talks.

This isn't the only serious conversation you guys are going to have to have. Not even close. At some point, you'll have to discuss fears, marriage, mother-in-laws, money, sex, and much, much more. And starting off in a place of honesty and openness only sets the tone for those future talks.

If you have a closed-door policy about past issues or feelings, that does not bode well for facing future obstacles together.

Create a culture of tolerance. Learn from each other. Trust each other. And talk about things that are scary. This is how you two become a united front. It's hard at first, but the more you share and the more you listen, the easier this gets. You only stand to benefit from it.

Now that you are on your way to becoming the best couple in existence, you might want to check out a few qualities that I have complied over the years after working with numerous and numerous girls in relationships. I've come to see that there are certain qualities that are in every healthy relationship, and I figured you could take a look to see if you can mirror some of these qualities in your relationship.

Here are a few healthy qualities I have found in successful couples:

They're not afraid to fight.

Oh yeah, successful couples definitely fight. Definitely. And they aren't afraid of it one bit. Because what successful couples know that most others don't, which is that arguing has some pretty awesome benefits.

First, more arguing means less secrets. If a couple doesn't argue, then one would assume there is nothing to actually argue about. Guys...how is that possible?

If you are a dating another human being, you are bound to get annoyed, curious, angry, insecure, or SOMETHING, right? Being open with your partner will naturally lead to arguments, small or humongous, and that's totally expected. Sometimes you have to get it out in order to move forward. So if you aren't arguing, then you're probably holding some stuff in. Some secret stuff.

More times than not, secrets are lethal in relationships. I mean, just turn on any movie with a romantic story line and wait for Act III, and you'll see. Secrets suck. It forms a huge wedge right between you and your partner that is borderline impossible to fix.

That's why arguing helps shove any hidden feelings out into the spotlight and acknowledges them. Once everything is left out in the open...the only way to move, is forward. And, wouldn't ya know it, all of those small problems vanish.

Arguing also creates honest dialogue for feelings.

Being open is also super beneficial in relationships (and the sky is blue!). But for real, letting the other person know how you feel is pretty vital, because that's how relationships move from scary to merry.

Expressing yourself, even if it's not necessarily in a calm

fashion, can do more for your relationship than you think. Of course, in a perfect world, we would all be calm 100% of the time and maturity would flow through the faucets in the form of wine. But, alas, that's not the case.

Let go of the shameful fear of being "that girl"—the needy, emotional, hot mess, and accept the fact that you are human who has a right to be heard. Or share. Or whatever else. Go about it in the right way, (owning your feelings, calmly speaking, a gentle introduction), and arguing could actually become tolerable.

At least you'll be solving some issues instead of throwing socks at each other. (I am a different person now, ok?)

Lastly, arguing creates a wonderful opportunity to set new boundaries.

When you argue, there is a high chance that both of you will suck at it. Normal. BUT—that means there is a huge window for making things better. Arguing gives you both the opportunity to take mental notes of how your relationship operates during fights. What are your triggers?

For some, it might be name-calling. Others might have certain taboo topics they don't like thrown in their face. A lot of people don't like being talked down to. Whatever it is, you'll probably notice that you get WAY more upset when the trigger is presented.

So, talk about it. Take the opportunity to set boundaries. What is ok to say, and what isn't? What sets the other one off into a tizzy? What sends you off into a spiral? Or, simply put, how would you guys "like" to fight? Let's list some examples of boundaries. Not leaving the room might be a good boundary. Or counting to five before speaking. (Yes I'm serious.)

Whatever it is, respect you and your partner's wishes. Arguing can be super productive if you let it be, but you have to work on it first. And it's all about da respect. Listen, be heard, and then you kiss. La dee dah.

So....yep, arguing is probably the main reason why happy couples also aren't afraid to exclaim, "RELATION- SHIPS TAKE FREAKING WORK."

They apologize and bounce back quickly.

Although happy couples aren't afraid to spend a night hashing it out, they also bounce back at an exceptionally fast rate. There's no grudge holding, no pouting, no resentment, and definitely no rebound fight introducing itself around 10 pm on a Saturday night. (Gah, those are the worst).

Successful couples honestly don't have time for that. They know that when a fight is over, it's time to say sorry and get on with their lives. Fighting clean is very helpful in these situations—so no name-calling, no bringing up the past, no contempt or mocking.

Apologizing is also incredibly important to establish respect, empathy, problem-solving, and the fact that they were LIST-EN-ING. They don't skip over it, that is, unless they want to keep goin' at it. And once those two golden words are out of the way, it's a fun Saturday night all over again.

They speak their truth.

While keeping the other person's feelings in mind, these couples aren't afraid to speak pretty dang honestly with one another. They have made an agreement that they can share their needs and wants without a huge steaming side of defensiveness. This doesn't mean they have to tell each other EVERY SINGLE DETAIL OF EVERY SINGLE THING…but it does mean that they feel comfortable in sharing whatever they need to.

They take care of themselves.

Whether they see a relationship counselor together, or they seek out their own individual method of self-help, they get it done. Self-care is definitely a top priority for a successful relationship because two fractions of a people cannot make a full relationship. You both have to be actively working on bettering yourself in order to make this work.

For real, every successful couple knows that the best way to take care of each other is to take care of themselves.

They don't let the past get in the way.

Successful couples might know all about each other's exes and crazy experiences and not so flattering episodes…but they certainly don't hold it against each other. They appreciate each other's exes. Yes, really. They appreciate that these people molded their partners into the people they are today.

And…well…also…there's that little chance that exes make us look like rock stars. There's no need to bash exes, women need to support one another, but if you are practicing all of those fabulous habits for building a healthy relationship, chances are, you are going to look like a diamond in the damn sky from here on out. Own it.

It's just so important for successful couples to not spend their relationship in the past. They choose to be secure in their current relationship because looking backward is only going to throw this relationship off balance.

They take five.

Although physical space usually isn't up for grabs, alone time is. During heated conversations, long vacations, or any other moment that might merit some alone time, they jump at it. They realize although it's healthy to be together, it may not be healthy to be together 24/7. Cause otherwise, they would most likely want to pull their hair out every other second.

On another note, it's not lost on successful couples that most likely, one is probably an introvert and one is an extrovert. That's typically how it goes. So, they embrace their personalities without letting it offend the other. The introvert is allowed to skip the party while watching *The Mindy Project* (that would be me) while the extrovert can go to the party without feeling like they're leaving the other behind. They can do their own thing without a giant, soul shattering fight. And it works. Swimmingly.

They don't help shame.

Successful couples gratefully accept help in any way, shape or form. When one partner offers to help the other, there isn't any "help shaming." Help is accepted at all times and forms because it's nice. Successful couples realize that help shaming creates resentment and oddly enough…little desire for the other to help. Imagine that! So, if one offers to help do the dishes, you ignore the soap still lingering on the plates. If one makes the bed and forgets the decorative pillows, you will survive.

Just remember cute little Rachel trying to make her trifle but accidentally halving it with shepherds pie. Did her Friends eat it? Well, Joey did, but the rest sure as hell pretended to. And that's because she contributed and gave it her all. So when you see the same gesture from your partner, you gobble it right on up!

They speak each other's Love Language.

Now, even though I recognize that love languages are a bit pop culture, they still hold some truth. To summarize quickly—here are the Five Love Languages by Gary Chapman, accompanied by examples:

1. **Words of Affirmation**
   Compliments—you are so smart, you look pretty, you're so talented...!
2. **Acts of Service**
   Tasks—taking out the trash, picking one up from the airport, cleaning the house
3. **Receiving Gifts**
   Presents—giving gifts, regardless of monetary value or meaning
4. **Quality Time**
   Date night—individual time together without distractions
5. **Physical Touch**
   Cuddling, hand holding, kissing, intimacy

Even though pretty much everybody likes all five languages, we tend to prefer one or two over the rest. Successful couples know their partner's love language and try very hard to practice it.

Hardly ever do partner's love languages match, so it's important that they understand their own, but adjust their actions to reflect their partner's.

If you've gone through this chapter and can confidently say your partner is a great source of happiness, support, and empowerment for you—try your hardest to incorporate healthy habits into your relationship. Be kind. Be honest. Be grateful. If you can do those things, you guys will be just fine.

When I get lonely these days, I think: So BE lonely, Liz. Learn your way around loneliness. Make a map of it. Sit with it, for once in your life. Welcome to the human experience. But never again use another person's body or emotions as a scratching post for your own unfulfilled yearnings.

—Liz Gilbert

Far too many people are looking for the right person, instead of trying to be the right person.

Gloria Steinem

13

Appreciating your Relationship Status

Full disclosure: If you are hitched or in a full bloomin' relationship, this section isn't for you. For the rest of you, follow along in a single file line. (Get it?) (I'm sorry my puns are terrible and insensitive.)

I'm going to say it: the quarter-life crisis can easily be spurred by being single. I know, I know, I know. We are FEMINISTS. We are FIGHTERS. We need a man like a fish needs a bicycle! (Thank you Irina Dunn for that absurdly bizarre quote!). But the reality is, we're also human. It's normal to want to be in a healthy relationship. But it's not normal to want to be in a relationship just for the sake of being in a relationship.

You are always going to like the idea of being with another human. It will always be lovely to have one human who we could play with whenever we wanted. **Especially right now.** Because right now totally sucks, and to have that one special someone whisper in our ear that we are special in every way…well. That would be peaches.

So let's get one thing straight: **you are single by choice.** Yep.

You are actively choosing this relationship status. And I refuse to change my mind about it. (Don't be mad at me!).

This theory came about on one particularly uneventful Sunday afternoon. I was sipping rose with my super hipster LA friends who are two of the most interesting human beings you will ever meet in your life. Naturally we went to an east side wine bar, because that's what people who can pull off fedora hats or jumpsuits or suspenders do. Honestly I'm like 99% sure you can't gossip about pop culture east of Vermont Avenue, so our only option was to start philosophizing about life and all its mysteries. When in Rome.

It went a little something like this:

What does it mean to have free will? How does it manifest in our lives? What does it mean to not have free will? Are most things in life pre-determined? Are we just reacting to stimuli subconsciously? Or are we actively making decisions and propelling ourselves along?

(boring boring boring boring boring)

To my delight things got a little...excited, and we maybe, or definitely, disrupted a few patrons' scrabble games. It ended up being split right down the middle—team free will vs. team pre-determined, but what we all agreed on is how important it was to believe that we have free will. Without the **belief**, the world would be chaos.

It should be no surprise that I cheered exuberantly for team free will. I think we make decisions every day that steer our lives forwards or backwards. I hope we aren't simply responding to external stimuli or going through the motions on a daily basis because as *Game of Thrones* puts it, the ink is already dry. (RIP Hodor.)

Good decisions reap good luck. Or at least that's how I see it. I guess without that belief, I wouldn't be very good at my job. This revelation was quickly followed by a session I had with one of my longtime clients (don't worry, she is totes cool with me writing about her).

Without going into crazy detail—this particular client is special. Very special. And she's just now coming to terms with it. Many men in her life have led her to believe otherwise for far too long, including her boyfriend of five years. Yes, five. He was terrible. He would talk down to her, make her believe she wasn't attractive, would actively talk to other girls in front of her...just the worst. The WORST.

So, a year and a half after she finally dumped that sack of smoking shit, she got her moment. Yes, it was the form of a text message. Yes, it was eighteen months too late. Yes, it didn't change the fact that he was still a moron. But still! She finally got to read the long awaited apology she deserved, and it came with way more empathy, understanding, and regret than I could have ever hoped for.

Most of us never get that moment. No matter how much we FREAKING deserve it, we don't get it. So the fact that she did made me want to do a thousand cartwheels.

But...something was still irking her. While I was throwing her a party from across the country, she was having doubts. Sure, she was totally revamping her life and finally chasing after what SHE wanted (trust me, it's not an easy transition!).

But she still felt like she was falling short in some way. Then it dawned on her. A light bulb moment. **She felt like because she wasn't in a relationship, her journey wasn't complete.**

She hadn't done enough, pushed enough, or moved forward enough to truly feel like she had overcome her shameful and passive past. All because she didn't have a fabulous boyfriend to prove that she had finally moved past that point in her life.

I understood why she felt this way; I just didn't agree that her relationship status had anything to do with her transformation. But how could I explain that to her? What was the underlying reason she wasn't in a relationship that she should be proud of?

Then, it dawned on me. It was my turn to have a light bulb moment: free will.

Being single is a choice!

In fact, I've actually only met a few women in my life who I truly believe are single NOT by choice. And they happened to be really, really mean. Like, really mean. Mean people don't make good life partners, so I figured that was the reason why. But for the other hundreds of single women I have met in the last few years, I have always assumed it was a choice. And I think I'm right.

For every woman out there, I believe this to be true:

If you wanted to be married, you could be.
If you wanted to be engaged, you could be.
If you wanted to be in a relationship, you could be.
Just as if you wanted to be single, you could be.

My client could have easily responded to that text message with open arms. She could have gotten back together with him in an instant. In six months, they could be engaged. In a year, they could be married. And soon after that, they could begin starting a family.

Would he still be a smoking sack of shit? You bet.

And that's not what she wanted. She wanted to be treated with respect. She wanted consideration. She wanted accountability. She wanted someone who saw her for who she in the present—not a year and a half later. And I'm betting you do, too.

Your relationship status is in your power.

I know some of you are thinking, "This is absolute bullshit. I really want to be in a relationship and no one wants to be in a relationship with me!" That's not true.

I guarantee you that you could be in a relationship with someone. There's probably someone from your past, a coworker, a classmate, a family friend, or an awkward acquaintance who would be more than happy to be in a relationship with you. Maybe you know this, or maybe you haven't given them the chance to declare it, but someone would like the opportunity.

The real question isn't who wants to be in a relationship with you, it's do you want to be in a relationship with them? **Being in a relationship means that you have found somebody you would rather spend time with more so than hanging out by yourself.**

And you know what? You're pretty awesome. You like good TV. You read intriguing books (like this one!). You eat delicious food. You scroll through interesting things on Facebook. You are a ridiculously hilarious Snapchatter. (OMG you are adorable with the puppy filter. Seriously.) And you are actively trying to better yourself. So honestly, this potential date better be *hella* exciting to beat all that.

I am very proud that my client is single. I think it shows strength, self-confidence, patience, and optimism. **If she had prioritized her relationship status over her happiness, she'd**

be dating some dude who doesn't value her time, commitment, kindness, or love. She would fall back into old habits. She would stop putting herself first. Instead she's staying single until she finds someone who supports her positive changes and pushes her to be even better.

If we are ready to be in a relationship, all that means is we are ready to be in a relationship with the right person. Because that's what we deserve, and nothing less. And finding the right relationship takes a lot time for a lot of people. It's not a sprint.

Yes, some people strike it out of the park in high school, and that's amazing...but most don't. I didn't. She didn't. There's a reason high school sweethearts are so revered. It's because it hardly ever happens! It's an exception! Most wait a while to find the right person because it takes time to get to know yourself, figure out your own life goals, and meet someone who compliments your hard work.

Funny enough (not like "haha" funny but more like eye roll funny) men don't really have to deal with any of this. The concept of being single doesn't seem to be an issue. Most people *assume* men are single by choice. They are "playing the field." They are "waiting for the right one." They are "focused on their career." But not women. Hell, if we used any of those excuses, we would be labeled as sluts, ugly, or bitches.

Yay.

Plus, women are mostly responsible for shouldering the blame for our relationship status, even if we are in complete control of it. A woman wanting to be single? The madness! No woman actually WANTS to be single! What else would she do with her time?! Make sandwiches FOR HERSELF?!

Breathe, Kali. Breathe.

Honestly it's fine, because these are typically the same

humans who don't realize "how are you still single, you're so cute!" is pretty offensive. My go-to line was usually "Yes I am cute and yes I am single and those are not mutually exclusive you asswipe."

I'll let you come up with your own line.

Or you can just not let those opinions bother you. Because if you believe in free will like I do, then you know it's pretty obvious that you could be in a relationship if you wanted to be. But instead you are making good decisions for yourself by prioritizing your own happiness before your relationship status. It's not pathetic or desperate or lame to admit that in a perfect world you would like to have a companion. That's human nature. Everyone on this planet would like a partner who just gets them...but not all of us are diligent enough to do the self-work in order to be ready for a relationship like that, or patient enough to wait for it.

You are.

Moral of the story? Create space for someone who matters. Let yourself be open to the opportunity of a truly inspiring relationship—*but nothing less*. Be bold enough to not apologize or be ashamed of dating yourself. You're pretty amazing. And if you can find someone who tops your "me time," then so be it. And if you don't, that's great too. Because having a boyfriend is not a requirement for living a fulfilling life.

But chances are, you probably will meet someone. It's just simple math. Most people couple up at some point in their lives. So in the meantime, let's take advantage of this time. You are free of the responsibilities and the obligations a relationship brings, so now is the time to focus on yourself.

I know, learning to appreciate being single is about as difficult as learning to see the forest through the trees. Sometimes it feels like it can't happen—especially when you consider your-self to be a "relationship person." It almost feels like a part of you is missing even though you know that's absurd logic.

Or maybe you might really like being single. Perhaps you have cracked the code and found out that being single is like the best thing EVER and you aren't sure you want it to end. If that's you, brava. Seriously. You are a queen.

If it's not, don't beat yourself up. But instead of dwelling on your lack of a plus one, focus on taking advantage of the time you have by yourself so you can be 100% ready to roll when you do find your certain special human. You'll BOTH be much better off.

This is my philosophy on how to take advantage of being single:

Get in the habit of being selfish.

Yup. I said it. I want you to be selfish. Like so selfish that Santa brings you the entire coal mine instead of a few dirty bundles. Get in the habit of putting yourself first now, because trust me, once a romantic interest comes along, that is going to go flying out the window.

Before we go crazy, I don't want you to become some troll who is only out for herself. But I do want you to really focus on asking yourself "What do I want?" first.

When you are in a serious, committed relationship with someone, you have to ask not only what YOU want, but you also have to consider someone else's opinions, desires, and needs. That's what solid relationships are built on. So when you are not in a relationship, take sweet, sweet advantage.

I want you to have a pulse on how you want your state of

events to unravel. Instead of "going with the flow" or deferring action to others, take it upon yourself to cultivate some strong opinions. Get a sense of what you like and how you like it. Don't be afraid to put yourself out there.

Not everyone might like it, but as we've already covered, you don't have to date them. Or be friends with them. You were not put on this planet to be liked. You were put on this planet to live. And living involves being selective with how you spend your time.

If you don't need convincing to be opinionated, that's awesome. Dig in, girl. This is your shining moment. In fact, this is what pure FREEDOM feels like you. Don't restrain yourself—get used to speaking your voice and coming into your own. Because once you find somebody you truly love, you will naturally want to share the spotlight and listen to their opinions. And you will be very susceptible to losing your identity. It just happens. So exercise your voice, your opinions, and your determination as hard so you can right now so that if a relationship does introduce itself, you have a firm hold on who you are and what you want.

Develop personal hobbies.

Other than the dreaded question, "are you seeing anybody?" I would have to say the second most anxiety-provoking question is probably "what do you like to do for fun?"

Write self help books..

OMG *panic*

My life is boring.

What a downer. It's mildly humiliating when you don't have a few go-to answers to this question at your holiday office party, so now is the time to get going. Everyone needs some personal hobbies. Something to get that creative energy out. Yes, mine so happens to be writing (le duh). I like to write, a lot. And writing is a pretty solidary activity. It's all mine. I don't share the process with anybody, only the results.

Yes, it's nerdy, but it's my thing.

So what do you like to do that's all yours?

I want you to come up with a few personal hobbies that you are able to do all by yourself. It's ok if the hobby might intrinsically be a social endeavor. For instance, I know a lot of film buffs who proudly say going to the movies is their favorite hobby. It's so LA. I love it. My only issue with it is when they refuse to go alone.

Have you ever been to a movie alone? It's amazing. No one talks to you, no one looks at you, no one sits next to you, and no one whispers in your ear "Oh my God look at Liam Hemsworth—do me" while drooling on your recently purchased faux cashmere sweater. Instead you get pure silence and pure focus. It's a magical thing.

So my point is, develop a hobby regardless if you feel awkward doing it alone. You deserve to have an individual passion that requires permission from NOBODY to execute. And you will be much better for it when the time comes for you to invite somebody into the space with you. That is, if you want to.

Work on your friendships.

This is another negative side effect of relationships: they tend to put a little strain on friendships.

It's not that your friends all of a sudden hate you just because you get a significant other and it's not because you will start hating your friends, either. It's because your time will be cut in half.

It starts with the weekends. They'll bring you to a wedding, you'll bring them home to meet the parents, then there are date nights and cuddle nights and Netflix nights…and then, dang. When are you supposed to hang with your friends? You're still a regular at Bachelor Mondays and Wine Wednesdays, but it's not like it was before.

Before we continue, I just have to get this out there: You are NOT going to lose your friends. I repeat, just because you have a relationship does NOT mean you lose you friends.

But it is in your best interest to double down on those friendships while you can.

You and your friends are going to be pulled apart in different directions. People get jobs and promotions and have to move as a result. They decide to go back to their hometowns to settle down. And they will definitely meet a special someone and start producing an insanely cute yet very time consuming family.

This doesn't mean that the love you share with your friend group goes away, and it doesn't mean the time you have together is any less special. But as you get older your schedule will probably get more crowded, so you have to make sure you are spending an inordinate amount of time sealing these friendships for life.

Trap those girls, you hear me? Trap 'em good.

Focus on what you'd like to change.

Again, the amount of free time in your life is going to drastically change when you enter into a serious relationship. I don't care how independent, feminist, or anti-love you are – that is what happens. You are going to be confronted with a person so fabulous that you actually aren't going to get sick of hanging out with them every single day!

I know! It's seriously crazy.

So in the meantime, get your accomplishment ducks in a row.

I love the Mindy Kaling quote at the beginning of this chapter because it's so freaking true. Most of the time when we feel down about ourselves for not having a relationship is when the other parts of our life are crumbling. So the best remedy to loneliness isn't actually finding a relationship—it's self-care.

I don't know about you, but I like my self-care with a little ambition on the side.

I'm all about baths (no I'm actually not, I can't sit in my own filth for that long) and romantic comedies and working out (if you count dancing) and whatever else gets you to relax and focus on YOU—but I like when there is a reward at the end. Something that is permanent. Something like a degree or a product or a service. Something that you can get lasting results from. Something that you're proud of.

Maybe that's working on your health and fitness. Maybe it's going back to school. Maybe it's starting up that side hustle you always said you'd try. Whatever it is, do it now. Trust me, it is better to change your life before you start dating someone seriously. Because when that happens, you will always want to take them into consideration. Always.

You are free right now. Free as a bird. As much as I know that might possibly pain you, it is the best gift you could ask for right now at your age. You have the time you need to craft the life you want, and then when you meet the right person, it will feel like the timing could not have been better.

Date.

Not to like, find the one. Not yet. They will introduce themselves whenever you're ready. But don't shy away from dating just to date.

Here is my take on dating: it is super intimidating, super nerve-wracking, it can be incredibly awkward, and it is a necessity of life.

Think of it this way: you probably don't like job interviews, but you also probably wanted a job. And it would have even been smart of you to go on job interviews when you didn't even really want the job. Why? To practice. To get better at your interviewing skills so when a job you actually WANTED became available, you were ready. Game freaking on.

Same goes for dating. In fact, not only does "practice dating" help for the real deal, it also teaches you to become more selective. If you don't date, then your dating pool is everybody. And if your dating pool is everybody, you are not going to find the right person for you. Trust me on that. You need to be selective with a capital S before you clear the bench. So go out on a few dates. Take inventory. See what you like. More importantly, see what you DON'T like. And continue to gather information until you can hone in on exactly what you're looking for, whether that's for the night, or forever.

14

Finding the Right Relationship

So ok. You're fine with being single. In fact, you're great with it. You have realized that there are plenty of eligible bachelors lined up out your door ready to make your damn day but you simply aren't interested. And perhaps you haven't met the man of your dreams yet. But you are sophisticated, interesting, and fucking fabulous so you are totally cool with waiting for the one.

But it still kinda irks you. And it irks you...that it irks you. **But it's not wrong to want to be in a relationship.**

I know a lot of single women. They roam the streets of LA, they're my clients on Blush, and some are my close friends. And that's to be expected. I'm in my late twenties, and the average age for marriage is crawling closer and closer to that 30-year mark. So to me, it's pretty standard—even healthy—that a solid amount of my network is not in a relationship.

However, I'm noticing more and more each month that my amazing, fabulous, independent, rock star girls feel that it's TOTALLY wrong to *want* to be paired off. It's like wanting to be in a relationship is a shameful endeavor—meant for only the weak. The girls who are paired off, well, they're great because they already found someone. But anyone who is actively searching, or even vocal, about wanting to be settled with a romantic partner is pathetic.

And that is just such bullshit.

Here's the skinny: humans are designed to attract a partner. It's part of life. The planet won't populate itself, amiright? Of course, there are plenty of social constructs we have evolved past—so I am totally down with the reality that not all of us want to get married or have babies. If that's not your jam—I'm all for it. But for the rest of us, being or wanting to be in a relationship doesn't mean you are clingy, pathetic, weak, or dependent.

It means you are human.

So here are some pointers and reasons for why it is NOT wrong to want to be in a relationship.

1. You are not weak if you feel lonely.

I know we are in an age of extreme independence and female power, which I love. Really, really, L-O-V-E.

However, it does come with a few negatives. Not many, but a few. Mainly, I've noticed this independent streak has created the complex "you are weak if you want a significant other."

Not "need"—notice that?—**WANT** a significant other.

That is exceptionally unfair. Honestly, no one I know *needs* a partner. My single clients are exceptionally fulfilled on their own. My single friends fill their calendars effortlessly and are seriously soaring. But do they want a relationship? Probably! Why? Because participating in a happy and healthy relationship is a normal goal.

Just to be clear, the main difference between needing and wanting a relationship can be answered in two questions:

1. Do you skip out on life events because you don't have a significant other? **Warning sign.**
2. Do you participate in life alone, but would like a buddy to share it with? **Winning.**

Easy. So if you are living a normal, fulfilled, reasonably happy life right now, then you don't *need* a partner. If you feel lonely on Sunday nights or wouldn't mind having a permanent date to bring to a wedding, then you are preparing yourself towards a very healthy, balanced, relationship.

You are also not an anti-feminist if you want someone to cuddle with, laugh with, or to kiss under the mistletoe.

It is impossible to think that we will never WANT another person. So, if you are critically worried about your state of independence, ask yourself these questions. (P.S.—these are good to ask if you are single or in a relationship!):

1. Do I have a support group?
2. Am I chasing my dreams?
3. Are my finances in order?
4. Do I have personal hobbies that I enjoy?
5. Am I a participating member of society?

If you answered "yes" to all of those, you are in fabulous shape.

2. Blame evolution.

For. Real.

It's as simple as this: **Most of us are hardwired to seek out a**

mate. Our bodies need two to tango. Doesn't matter if you are straight, gay, bi, or pan—our hormones are telling us to gravitate towards another person. The only exception I have ever found is asexuality. Otherwise, it's just a chemical thing. It doesn't even matter if our partners stay afterward—because, voilà!—we are set to rebound and find someone else. That is the way we were made. And it's a beautiful thing.

So as much as you might want to blame your cognitive functions for luring you into the arms of another, you really can't. Your hormones are responsible for that. After all, we are still animals—even if we like to forget it sometimes. Our instincts are going to be stronger than our thoughts because that's how we developed in the first place. Literally, we came from organisms that did not have a prefrontal cortex. For years we roamed the earth as walking impulses just ready to procreate. So stop being so hard on yourself over something you can't even control. You were made to love.

But—just for the record—this is NOT an excuse to stay with shitty people. Evolution isn't a cop out for remaining in a terrible relationship. But it is a very real biological explanation for why we crave attention, why we have desires and why we will NEVER go an entire lifetime without wanting someone else to share our lives with. We may not crave the same person for our entire lives, or maybe even for a year, but our bodies will always provide us with an itch for someone else. And there's really nothing you can do about it.

2. Mates are a lovely bonus.

You do not need a partner/girlfriend/boyfriend/husband/wife

to **survive** in life, but it is nice to **share** the ups and downs with someone.

But you already know this. Most of you have gone through a breakup before. They feel like death, don't they? You can't breathe, your anxiety spikes, you can't sleep, eating is a chore—it's terrible. You doubt that you will ever feel happiness ever again.

However, you survived. You are still alive, putting one foot in front of the other, and living your life.

So this just proves that relationships in life are bonuses. They are not meant to sustain us. Great partners challenge us, grow with us, embrace us, do not hold us back AND have their own life. **Relationships make life exciting—but they don't make life exist.**

So the question is, why wouldn't you want that bonus?

It seems silly not to be open to it. In fact, it feels backward. You'd go for a cash bonus at work. You'd go for bonus points on a test. You'd go for a free drink at a wine bar (as long as it's not fucking Merlot). But you wouldn't go for the life bonus of finding a significant other? That doesn't make much sense.

Finding a relationship is a healthy way to live a balanced life, and don't let anyone tell you otherwise (including yourself).

4. In the meantime, practice autonomy dates.

If you're tired of feeling lonely but want to put that energy to good use, go on some autonomy dates.

It's simple. Spend some time investing in you, and make it fun. Seriously! Take yourself on a date! Go spend some time with nature, pack yourself a romantic picnic and fill it with everything you like: cheese, wine, more cheese, some more wine, and cheesecake. Perfection.

Just don't punish yourself because you aren't in a relationship. You can do all of the fun "couple" things by your damn self. This is one of the lovely side effects of feminism that I am fully embracing – no shame whatsoever.

Ok, so now that we have decided that being single is awesome and that there are ways to fully unlock the beauty of its bounty, we can talk about what it looks like to find the right relationship.

But…how? I'll put it simply.

Your vibe attracts your tribe.
Your view attracts your boo.
Your maturity attracts your security.

Poetry may not be my gift, but damn was that fun.

Moving along.

There's a reason we meet certain people at certain times. I'm not going to get too spiritual on you—but I do believe in attraction and energy. You get what you put out—or something eerily like it. Life is a constant balancing act, and we are subconsciously trying to find ways to balance ourselves out through someone else or something else. This is the same reason introverts and extroverts gravitate towards each other—they balance out their social energies through each other.

So what does this mean, and how does this play into attraction? A few things.

I believe that in order to attract a suitable person for you, you need to be a suitable person yourself. And the best way to achieve that is to chase balance all by yourself. Luckily, we have covered that extensively, so you are already on track. And no, it's not the most glamorous or exciting endeavor out there, but it might just guarantee a much better life partner in the long run.

This is my best advice on how to attract the right partner for you once you are ready:

Focus on emotional stability.

Notice how whenever you feel desperate for connection, you're living in an emotional ghost town? This isn't an accident.

Again—remember—life is a balancing act. If you have all of the emotions bursting out of you at any given moment, you are going to attract someone who can barely identify what it feels like to be happy. You are giving off vibes that you are out of sync, and your natural romantic partner will be someone who evens you out.

But that's not what you want. If you are emotionally charged, you are going to want someone who wants to discuss those emotions. And that will absolutely not happen. Emotionally stunted people don't want to talk about feelings. They can barely comb out jealousy from anger, so you are going to be bursting at the seams with frustration and pent up energy. And that leaves you in a bit of an uncomfy spot.

In order to find someone who is emotionally available to you—you must be emotionally stable yourself.

Do not (subconsciously) search for someone to balance you out. Instead, learn to identify, understand, and process your emotions individually. Build your emotional resilience. Feel everything you possibly can, and adopt coping and processing skills to make the task easier. The better you get at processing feelings yourself—the more stable you will become and less dependent you will be on anyone else for emotional security.

The right partner will be your equal, not your balancing act. You can still be sensitive. You can still have emotions. But you won't be depending on anyone else to handle them for you.

Focus on happiness.

Aside from emotional stability, in order to attract an optimistic, confident, happy person—we ourselves need to be—you guessed it—optimistic, confident, and happy.

This can be difficult, especially when you are sick and tired of being single. It's easy to slip into negative self-talk and pessimistic thinking. You start to believe that you actually deserve to be alone—otherwise, you would have somebody.

But that is not true. Being single is less about a lack of relationship with somebody else and more about the relationship you have with **yourself**. You have time to heal yourself from any past heartbreak. You have time to get to know yourself and focus on your wants and needs. You have time to start putting yourself first. And most importantly, you have to start having your own back. Until you do those things, you won't be truly happy.

Attracting happiness.

I also believe it is possible to attract good things into our life. **Part of being happy is simply being delusional.** It sounds weird, but here's an example:

Let's say something bad happens. You don't get the job you really wanted. Your rent gets jacked up and you are forced to move. You and a friend have a falling out. All of these things suck. Some people will wallow in the misery and wonder, "why me?" They will pick apart the facts until they can prove that they deserved all of this bad stuff. They will excitedly play the victim. And for some reason, more bad things start to snowball. Otherwise known as the quarter-life crisis.

Some will strive to find the silver lining. They will actively try to find a positive perspective to protect themselves from falling victim to irrational negative thinking. They know that plenty of reasons could be behind the negative setback—but that choosing to believe the least destructive theory only stands to benefit their mental health.

And wouldn't you know it? Their mantra "this wasn't the right opportunity for me" turns into landing an even better job the following month. They're reasoning of "perhaps it was simply time to move" turns into them securing an incredible apartment and meeting fabulous new neighbors. And coincidentally or not, that "friend" they were fighting with turned out to be a pretty terrible person. That fight was actually their escape from an abusive situation, and they are grateful for it.

Sure, maybe all of it is delusional. But I'll be damned if it doesn't work. Because the people who adopt these self-preserving tricks are the ones who seem way happier in life.

So try it out. You have the time right now to now focus on yourself, your thought processes, and your theory of happiness. Start cheering yourself on from the inside. Be your own advocate. Have your own back. Create a positive environment for you to explore. **And instead of focusing on your future part-ner—focus on yourself.**

This is how you are going to inevitably attract the right partner for you—because if you are happy—you will attract more happy things. With that kind of thinking, a bad date is now a *great* thing because you are still available to meet someone worthy of your time instead of being tied down to an asshat who made you feel bad about your career choice.

Honestly, like how fucking dare he? Happiness breeds more happiness. Happy people hang around other happy people. **Your vibe attracts your tribe.**

Be happy with yourself. Other happy beings will pick up on it and come running. And when that happens, it will simply be a **bonus** to your complete life. One that you'll deeply cherish.

Focus on growth.

Movement attracts other movement. So if you are moving forward, you will attract someone else's forward movement. And if you're regressing…well. You can only imagine what that will attract.

Time is going to pass regardless of what you choose to do with it. I personally am in favor of growth. And I think your future relationship can only stand to benefit from growth as well. But you have to take action NOW in order to see results LATER.

Trust me, relationships can function when they are regressing, standing stationary, or progressing. You two can be buried in your pasts—ruminating over "what could have been," creating unnecessary jealousy and avoiding future plans. You can be happily positioned in the present—living every moment as it comes and not worrying about what's ahead. Or, you can have your eyes set on the future, and making sure your "now" counts for tomorrow.

What kind of relationship do you want?

I'm biased, but I would like the third for all of you. At least, if a serious relationship is what you are gunning for. Otherwise, you'd probably be happy as a peach with door #2 (and forget about commitment). But if you want to find someone to build a future with, then you need to start building one for yourself today. Send it out into the universe—and you'll be tickled pink with what comes back.

Remember, being single is a choice, and it is most likely the best choice for you right now. You are strong enough, brave enough, smart enough, and resilient enough to tackle this quarter-life crisis without a partner in crime.

And if it's any consolation, I am definitely in your corner, cheering you the whole way through.

Part 5

How to Conquer Your Quarter-Life Crisis

15

Getting to Know Yourself

First thing's first: the quarter-life crisis is going to hit even the most self-assured individuals. You are not weak or pathetic or average because it's hit you, too. It knows no bounds. It's going to cause you to doubt yourself in ways you never even thought possible. You were probably once a very confident young person—ready to take on the world and completely convinced you were going to achieve everything you had your eye on.

You're not crazy for having this big of a 180. So I am going to help you brush up on some skills that you have put on the back burner for a while.

First, I have a question for you.

Do you know yourself?

Yes, I know you can name your favorite color. I know you can pick your favorite brunch spot and your most beloved film choice. You can articulate your political views and you can gracefully identify which fashion trends you think fit your style.

But still. Do you really know yourself? And if you do, are you comfortable expressing yourself unapologetically? This is where things get tricky. In order to figure out where you want to go, you have to figure out who you are right now in this moment. You are probably in the throws of developing some stronger, more developed opinions. You don't have to be the same person you were when you were 18.

In fact, please don't be.

You have to double down on getting to know the real you outside of the context of someone else. For the majority of your life, you have gotten to know yourself through heuristics. You assume you like something because your family and friends like something. You listen to how others gauge a certain issue or topic, and you try on their opinion for size. It's not an unreasonable way to navigate yourself—other people are our basis of normalcy.

But not anymore. Instead of using others as our gauge, you are going to follow these steps to form your own opinions and vocalize them as you see fit. Here's how to get started.

Create Space

The first step to tuning into your inner self is to create space from others. If it sounds cold—don't worry—you're not going to cut out any of your healthy relationships.

Think of it this way: in order to hear a whisper, you have to step away from any loud noises. That's common sense. You don't run away from the noise or yell at the noise or never want to hear a loud noise again. You just have to tune it out for a second to hear the soft, yet exceptionally important, whisper.

You are the whisper.

And more than likely, the loud noises are a combination of others' opinions that you have valued for quite some time. This practice typically starts at a young age, especially for young people pleasers. Why insert yourself when you could listen to others' opinions and create harmony? It made sense then, and sometimes it still makes sense now. The problem is when we habitually forget to listen to ourselves.

So, in order to figure out what you really think about things, you have to create a little space.

You don't have to bounce ideas off of people. You don't have to "run things by" your friend. You don't even have to say what you're thinking out loud. You just have to give yourself enough space from others to cultivate your own opinion on matters.

If it feels like you're keeping secrets, that's fine. Perhaps a little more privacy will do you some good. You aren't being manipulative or sneaky or dishonest. You're just keeping your opinions in a safe space until they are ready to be released out into the real world.

The single most important part of creating space is figuring out how you feel BEFORE letting someone else's contribution in. You are free to change your mind if others make valid points—that's how we learn and grow. But you should make it a habit of figuring out what you believe or think first as much as possible and then entering into a conversation with an open mind.

Try New Things

When we get in the habit of adopting others' opinions, it's easy to get in a comfort zone that isn't really even ours. We get the same nail color every time because dark purple nails "aren't classy" according to Mom. We opt for '80s classics because Dad really liked Tom Petty, even if deep down we're more partial to '90s pop. They might sound inane on paper, but who knows how often you are declining your own quiet opinions simply because someone else's is louder?

Deviating from the norm causes unwanted attention and questions. And if we don't know how we feel about things, how would we defend our choices anyway?!

You don't have to! That's the beauty of it all.

I dare you to try as many new things as possible and not worry about the consequences of each choice. Paint your nails sparkly orange for all I care. Go crazy.

The longer you put off evaluating what you think and how you feel about new experiences and styles and trends, the more you are delaying getting to know the REAL you. Avoid the urge to ask somebody what they think about it first. Avoid the ping inside you whispering to get someone's permission. Don't. Act now and discuss later.

Warning: you probably won't like a lot of the things you try. Maybe dark purple nails really aren't your thing. But you know what? That's AMAZING because you came to that conclusion on your own instead of letting someone else decide for you. It doesn't matter if you turn out to be super picky or super laid back—as long as you have decided for yourself.

Disappoint Others

Let me start out with this adorable quote by Dita Von Teese:

> *You can be the ripest, juiciest peach in the world, but there will always be somebody who doesn't like peaches.*

So stinkin' cute.

If you are determined to really get to know yourself and push through this quarter-life crisis, then you ain't gonna please everyone. Not only are you going to have to go against others' opinions while trying to figure out your own, but you are also going to do the exact opposite of what someone you love would do. And in turn, you could disappoint them.

So do it. Disappoint the hell out of them.

It's not like you're intentionally hurting anyone. And yeah, it would be nice if others didn't care so much about how you lived your life. But they do. You're awesome. And people are always going to take interest in how you live your life. So, in order to shake off the pressure, you have to lean into your ways and be prepared to disappoint. You'll survive, and so will they.

Respect Others

You are going to be overcompensating for a lot of time spent agreeing with others. You are going to wake up one day and realize, you know what, you don't like cold weather. Or the Knicks. Or curling your hair. Or the color pink. And dammit, you're going to want everyone else to get on this bandwagon because you have finally seen the light!

But we still have to play nice.

It's easy to get caught up in this new bold, confident you. It's easy to start preaching, lecturing, and vehemently educating others so that they can get on board with your decisions. But that's not the way to go about it. (As I lecture you. Lolololol.)

Everyone has their own journey of self-development. You never know where someone else is in their transition of getting to know themselves. They might be just starting to form their own opinions, or they might have put a lot of hard work into figuring themselves out. We do NOT need to get in the way of that. Instead, be respectful of others' opinions regardless of where they are in their journey.

Remember, you probably found yourself on this path of self-discovery because you felt bullied, steamrolled, or suffocated to the point where you realized you HAD to stand up and figure out how you felt about things. So you don't want to be that bully to someone else. You can still have your principles, values, and opinions and respect others' of opposing views. In fact, respectfully disagreeing actually helps crystallize your judgments. Being able to openly consider another point of view in a calm and civilized manner and decide "Nah, not for me" is pretty dang mature.

16

Creating Positive Self-Care Habits

So now that you are working on pleasing yourself, we have to cut out that nasty habit of pleasing others.

Getting to know yourself will probably be reasonably fun—but tuning out the white noise of others expectations? This takes years—yes, years—of practice.

But man is it ever worth it.

You have to stop lighting yourself on fire to keep others warm. Right now you are "in" it. You are sculpting your life into the piece of art you've been dreaming of for years. But as you can see, it takes work. Living up to your own expectations is hard enough—we don't need the weight of others' designs for your life.

People pleasing is a toxic habit that will tear you apart if you don't begin eliminating it today. So here are some concrete steps to practice on a daily basis:

1. Assume it's not about you.

I know how it goes. You're beat bopping through the office,

super pumped about your recent progress review, and it happens. You make eye contact with Karen. Freaking Karen.

...and wouldn't you know, Karen's glance just doesn't feel right.

Is she pissed? Maybe she's jealous of my upcoming promotion. But like, what the hell did I ever do to her? Why would I deserve this kind of treatment? IT'S AN OUTRAGE I TELL YOU!

Ok, calm down there tiger. Let's give Karen the well-deserved break she deserves.

Maybe Karen is having a rough day. I hear she got dumped last night, stubbed her toe on the curb, drooled toothpaste all over her brand new floral blouse this morning, and her monthly package came a few days early. So yeah, Karen isn't quite winning at life right now. And that stare, well, it probs had absolutely nothing to do with you at all.

In fact, that look on her face was the result of her pondering over how she's going to tell her family she's coming to the family wedding sans one date.

Poor Karen.

If you constantly assume that every look, every comment, or every vibe has to do with you, then you are going to be swamped with people pleasing thoughts all day every day. Your brain is literally going to be consumed with what others are thinking and how you are going to fix some awkward scenario that doesn't actually exist.

So, instead, you have to assume it's not about you. Unless Karen comes up to you and calls you a tool bag to your face, you aren't allowed to react.

Not only does this behavior open up some space in your mind, but it also forces people to grow a pair if you actually DID do something to tick them off. If they want you to know how they feel, they're going to have to speak up. You catering to every glance, every tone, every hesitation—well, it just creates lazy entitled little monsters waiting to behave badly so you can come and fix it for them.

If they want you to cater to their needs, they're going to have to ask for it. Otherwise you're not wasting your time anymore.

2. Set goals.

I want some specific goals. I want some deadlines, I want some note taking, and I want some real concrete steps to get to these goals that you have decided to set for yourself.

Why? Because it takes the focus off of others and onto you.

So sign up for the GRE. Put paint on the canvas. Create a cover letter. Map out a business plan. Attend the event. Whatever it is that you have been putting off for all of the various reasons we manage to come up with, take action.

I want you to alter the question in your mind to "what do I want?" instead of "what do they want?"

Because trust me, you'll have a much better shot at happiness, and you won't inevitably turn into someone else's doormat. The difference between being a really nice person and a pushover (or selfish troll) is direction. You're going to be way too focused on accomplishing goals that you set for yourself to even consider bending over backward for someone else's goals.

And, just an FYI, this doesn't mean you are going to turn into an actual selfish troll. Promise. As I said earlier, I don't play like that. The key is, you can smile and wave and blow kisses to any person who crosses your path in life. They aren't interfering with your plan—your plan isn't dependent on anyone else, remember?

So, you can be nice. Being nice is cool. Being a doormat is not.

3. Play it out.

Ok, so let's say you get stuck in your cycle of people pleasing. Someone REALLY wants you to do something for them, and even though you know they are probably taking advantage of you, you simply feel so bad saying no. So play it out.

What's the worst thing that could happen? Really?

1. **You say no, and they talk bad about you.**

   Well, most likely everyone in their corner will find that pretty silly and not listen. People who bitch about other people not doing them favors probably don't get much airtime.

2. **You say no, and they ask someone else to do it for them.**

   Well this is AWESOME. They have found a new buddy to rely on! You are off the hook and have more time to focus on your own direction. Don't worry, it will feel uncomfortable at first, but you'll get used to being your own priority.

3. **You say no, and they get mad at you.**

   If you have someone who is going to throw a temper tantrum, you might want to friend new friends anyway. Plus, they can't get angry with you if they don't have an audience. So just collect your things and leave. They probably need to work that out on their own anyway.

4. **You say no, and they feel disappointed in you.**

   Simply explain to them that you don't have enough

216

time, and that you can't live life to please others. If anything, they should feel proud that you are sticking up for yourself.

If you come up with any other scenarios, do what we just did there. Play it out. And you'll see, it's much better to stick up for yourself than to exist to do favors for others.

4. Trim the fat.

If you constantly find yourself surrounded by people who need something from you, you could also couple working on yourself with trimming some individuals from your social circle. Don't be mistaken, though, I definitely think people pleasing is best fought off by setting clear boundaries for yourself, but I also think that sometimes we attract people into our lives who constantly encourage our people-pleasing behavior.

If you are noticing that a few particular members in your social crew tend to need everything from you, it might be time to reconsider the friendship. Friends should support each other—not suck out the life of each other. If that were the case we would be friends with vampires! (If only...). More on this later.

5. Manifest your future.

Make a vision board. Daydream. Manifest. Bring positive vibes to your future that don't have to do with ANYBODY else. What do YOU want? What kind of job do you want? Pet do you want? House do you want? Impact do you want? LIFE do you want? Think about it!

If we constantly attach our dreams to other humans, we will never get what we want. Other people are not in charge of our happiness. You are not in charge of other people's happiness. You are in charge of YOUR happiness. So let it go. Spend your time manifesting wonderful, amazing, bright things for yourself, and leave the others out of it.

Next, let's talk about comparing.

Let me guess—you logged onto Facebook, saw all of the pretty careers and pretty weddings and pretty babies, and cried yourself to sleep. (I don't know this from personal experience or anything…).

But you cannot compare the beginning of your journey to the middle of someone else's.

You have to stay focused on your own path, your own pace, and your own goals. Comparing is crap. It will only make you second-guess EVERY decision you've already semi-made-ish, and get you spinning in circles. You will never be able to achieve someone else's life, because that's not your purpose. Your purpose is to live your own. So here are some pointers on how to quit comparing and stay centered:

1. Catch yourself.

Seriously. It sounds lame, but hear me out. You need to actually focus on catching yourself comparing yourself to others every day. You will be amazed how often it happens! Because it happens like….all the time.

You are probably comparing your body to other bodies in your yoga class. I bet you try to calculate your salary compared to your buddies salaries just to make sure you feel extra shitty about your current job. You might even compare your apartment, your clothes, your makeup, your family, your relation-ship...the list goes on and on. And God KNOWS we compare how well liked we are in comparison to others (can that even be measured?)

So start paying attention to it. Now.

I swear, the more you catch yourself, the more you will be aware of the bad habit, and the more you can actively try to stop.

It's not like it's fun. It's not like you enjoy it. But once you are aware of this dirty habit, at least you'll know your triggers (when is it happening?) and your reactions (how does it make you feel?).

If you go through life unaware of bad habits, there's not a chance in hell you can do anything to stop them. Why would you? You don't even know you're doing them! So carry around a "comparison journal" for all I care and write down every time you feel "less than." Whatever you want your method to be, implement it every damn day.

2. Find perspective.

It's easy to beat yourself up for not being as far along in life as you wanted. I know when I was 16 I figured I would be married, own a house, be a dog mom, and have a crazy amazing job that paid me so much money I could buy whatever the hell I wanted—including the designer jeans that had the weird loops on the butt. All of my friends wore them and I still had no clue what the brand was. (Turns out they were Citizens—just figured that was pertinent information.)

Did that happen? Think we already covered that earlier.

Part of the reason I was probably so down on myself was

because I couldn't get this idea of what "success" looked like out of my head. And what's worse is that I decided to project that ideal onto everyone I saw around me. So guess what? Everyone who was married, owned a house, had a dog, or wore that silly unrecognizable brand of jeans was SO successful in my book. I had zero time to actually have a conversation with them and learn about their successes and struggles. Nah, I just jumped right on ahead into a major puddle of conclusions and assigned 'SUCCESSFUL' to their life status.

That was really not fair. I was assuming like crazy just to make myself feel even worse about myself. And the funny part was, a lot of these people had totally different definitions of success. They might have been looking at me thinking my life was glitter-glam perfect, and I was too ashamed to even notice.

I had to learn the hard way that everyone has their own path of getting somewhere. Your journey will not look like hers, and hers won't look like his, and his won't look like yours.

But furthermore, life doesn't unfold in a steady measure of accomplishments. We have spurts of amazingness in this year, a spiral of setbacks in that year, and a bunch of random mediocrity floating in the middle. You might be in a total slump when someone else is crawling out of their mediocrity bit and shooting to success at lightning speed. But you have no idea how long it took them to get there, how hard they have been working, and what they had to overcome earlier. You're just looking at their successes assuming it was easy for them. It hardly ever is. Your life will **never** look like anybody else's, no matter how hard you try. You might as well be comparing a panda bear to an elephant. Both super cute. Both super awesome. But comparing them makes zero sense. Find comfort in your own journey.

3. Express gratitude.

When you are forced to measure up your accomplishments and achievements in comparison to someone else, you should at least be positive, right? So offer yourself some gratitude. List out reasons why where you are in life is absolutely great. Maybe you are just starting out and you are really excited about where you are heading. Yay! Maybe you're making some awesome money right now. Peanut butter and jealous! Perhaps your love life is blossoming. Aww, romance. So schweet.

Whatever it is, express gratitude. Give yourself some positive feedback. Life hardly ever looks as perfect as we want it to, but there is always some good stuff there. So list them! Assure yourself that you have reasons to celebrate. If you do that, your life won't look so glum anymore.

4. Find encouragement.

Ok, so you accidentally got lost in the spiral of comparing EVEN though you caught yourself, desperately tried to find perspective, and listed off some items of gratitude. But for some reason, the itch to compare is still bringing you down.

Welp. Let's try something else. Take some comparison-triggers that are taunting you, and put them on your to-do list. Otherwise known as, **find encouragement from other people's successes.**

If appropriate, ask them to be your mentors. Be inspired by their work. Whatever it is, let their success further encourage you to keep going. There is room for everyone. Seriously. There are six billion people on this planet—there is no way one person is sucking up all of the room for you to shine.

That would be like Khloe Kardashian convincing herself all of the fame was already conquered by Kim. OMG that would suck. Life without Khloe? How would we survive? She's obvi the most relatable Kardashian by a mile.

Wait, but there's Kourtney, too.

And Kendall.

And…Kylie?

See? Those sisters didn't look at each other and think "Kim has already achieved what we want to achieve so FORGET IT I'm just going to sit in my room all day and do nothing."

Not even close. Instead, they worked together, found their own niche, and launched themselves into reality superstardom by being famous for just being themselves.

Talk about confidence.

Take away: When we're snooping on others' lives, we might as well take others' intimidating successes and turn them into motivation to do better.

5. Dream.

Yes—dream. The easiest of all the action items I am shoving down your throat. Thank goodness.

Comparing makes us feel pretty crappy about our current state of life, but understand that this moment is only temporary. You have so much time to push and mold your life into what you want it to be. Maybe you perceive that someone else's life is already happening, but your life is still in *development*. You still get the pot of gold at the end of the rainbow.

So…what DO you want it to be?

Let yourself explore your future without *confinements*. The beauty of a still-in-development life is that you get to fill in the blanks as you go. You can be creative and adventurous with how your life unfolds. And yes, someone might be living the exact version of your dream. But that's ok. In fact, it's perfect, because you get the rare chance of observing and learning from their mistakes while you're still figuring it out. Pretty amazing, actually.

So what if you stopped comparing, you feel like you know yourself, but you can't shake the feeling that you need to be perfect in every way possible? Then I would say you are probably normal, but that being a perfectionist will be the demise of any shot at conquering the quarter-life crisis. If you think about it, you and I have been trained to be perfect our whole lives. We went to school on time, never talked in class, got straight As on our homework, and were constantly reassured that we were doing a lovely job. This pattern followed us from elementary school to middle school and high school—and even into college. Maybe sometimes we exchanged our As for Bs in our tough classes, and occasionally we got grounded from time to time, but overall, "perfect" wasn't so hard to achieve.

And then we graduated.

Oy. What a blow. All of a sudden we need the perfect job, the perfect apartment, the perfect boyfriend, the perfect salary, and we needed it yesterday. Because that's how our life is supposed to unfold, right? High heels – high standards. The perfect girl's dream.

But it doesn't work like that. *Because* perfect *isn't real.* What we thought was "perfect," was really just us putting in some effort and getting some decent results. And honestly, the stakes really weren't that high. It was easy. We were given a formula, we were told how to succeed, and we followed the rules.

Plug and chug, girl.

But after school—our sacred formula disappeared. It just evaporated into thin air and left us alone and clueless. So now, it's our job to decide what "perfect" really means. And instead of creating that definition ourselves, we're looking to everyone else. And so, the rat race begins.

Society will always dictate some ridiculous standard of perfectionism. I can't control that, and neither can you. But we can try to fight it off to the best of our ability. So, here are some ways on how to stop being a perfectionist, and start being a happy human.

Appreciate the process.

You've heard it so many times—focus on the journey, not the results. But all you're really thinking when you hear that cliché is, "If I don't focus on the results, how can I even know what I'm working towards?"

Solid question.

What that quote really means is divide your attention between both the journey AND the results, and appreciate both aspects. If you get so caught up in the results that you don't even try to at least enjoy the process—you are wasting your time—and you are probably losing out on the opportunity to have the results you intended. Positive energy is required for positive results, so enjoying the process is crucial to the ending product.

But, there's also one more benefit to this strategy—and that's the element of **pride**. When you work hard for something, and you actually enjoyed it, you become **proud** of your result. And pride simply can't be measured.

Once you are proud of yourself and your creation, the idea of perfectionism doesn't seem as relevant anymore. Who cares if your home-cooked meal didn't turn out as well as Ina Garten's chicken florentine? You worked your damn ass off and it tastes pretty good, eh?

(I mean, it was ok. But whatever I made it all by myself.)

You may not be hitting it out of the park right now, but that doesn't mean your effort is for nothing. And that definitely doesn't mean you can't celebrate yourself. You have to give yourself credit because you are trying.

For God's sake, you're reading this book. If that isn't effort, I don't know what is.

So cultivate pride, and your lust for being perfect will slowly dwindle.

Mess up on purpose.

Or as I like to call it, exposure therapy.

When I was in grad school, I got a job as a server at a nice restaurant. I had probably applied to 200 different places of employment without so much as a "you suck and we aren't hiring you" reply, so waitressing was my last resort. I was determined to become good at this job so I could become somewhat financially secure—but also so I could prove to myself that I wasn't a total failure.

Now, this was not your average lunch spot. The cheeseburger cost fifteen dollars (um I could get a pedicure for that amount) and we turned tables so fast that my head would spin after a shift. I mean seriously if you are paying fifteen freaking dollars for a damn cheeseburger I would assume that these rich Dallasites would want to at least enjoy it—but no—they were on a mission to get in and get out.

This meant two things. One, I was going to make a ^$&# ton of money. And two, they expected the service to be **perfect**.

I remember on day two of my training, my boss asked me to carry three water glasses in one hand. If you don't know me, my hands are freakishly tiny. I was terrified. Like, this is not going to happen. I was going to spill everywhere. And get fired. And crawl in a hole. And never come out. And, bye.

I practiced and practiced and practiced. I had repeated nightmares of dropping all three glasses and spilling on myself, a coworker, or worse—a guest. The horror.

I ended up "failing" after three days of training. Yes, fail. They actually failed servers in training. The psychological torture that accompanied that lovely experience was humiliating, but nonetheless, I kept going and finally passed after two weeks.

My first real week on the floor, a tenured employee was watching me. I'm pretty sure she was worried I was going to scare the guests away since the look on my face was that of a clumsy girl in an egg and spoon race. So, on a crowded Tuesday lunch, she did what any smart human would do. As I rounded the upstairs corner, trying desperately not to drop three trembling glasses of water, she deliberately knocked them out of my hands. Glass shattered. I was soaked. She was smiling. Eyes were staring. And that was it.

There was a small round of applause from some smug table in the back (cannot STAND those people), but otherwise everything was fine. I think a few servers actually stepped over me to get to their next table. I quickly raced to the back, grabbed a mop, cleaned it up, and kept going. And after that, I wasn't so afraid of dropping the glasses anymore. Hell, it was almost an adrenaline rush.

If you are constantly worried about failing or falling short of your perfect standard, try the opposite. Mess up on purpose. You are resilient. You are designed to bounce back. So, you will.

Name one time you haven't been able to recover from something. One.

You can't. And I know that because you are still living and breathing and picking up the pieces right now as we speak. So if the fear of failure is so palpable that it's holding you back from just going for it—mess up on purpose. And you'll see, your ability to persevere will absolutely astonish you.

Play it out.

Yes, it's this game again!

If your situation doesn't really allow for the whole "mess up on purpose" strategy, that's fine. I get that you might not want to bomb your graduate school entrance exams on purpose. (In fact please don't because I don't want that kind of blood on my hands.)

Instead, ask yourself, "What's the worst that can happen?"

Seriously. What is the worst that can happen if what you are trying to achieve isn't perfect? So what you don't get into the graduate school you wanted. Are you going to die? Are you going to be shunned from society? Will your friends abandon you? Will you never be employed again?

I am going to guess the answers to those questions were a resounding NO. **Because your life isn't going to fall apart if you aren't perfect.**

In fact, the only one who will really freak out about falling short of perfection is you. And if anyone else cares THAT much about your accomplishments or shortcomings, could you please tell them to get a life? Or give me their number so I can tell them to get a life?

You are the only one who does and should care. You're also probably the only one who notices, for that matter. So relax and play it out. Ask yourself what would happen if you didn't reach your impossible standard. Answer honestly. And be specific. Go through every possible consequence that could arise, and then ask yourself how you would handle it and what you would do about it.

I used to do this all the time. In fact, I still do.

I started my company when I was just 25 years old. I didn't know anything about being an entrepreneur or running a business. And as much as I did know about counseling and helping clients, I wasn't an expert at it.

My biggest fear in the entire world was that it wouldn't work.

I had dreams that Blush was a terrible, horrible mistake. I was convinced it was going to tank and I was going to be so embarrassed because not only did I let my friends and family down who supported me throughout the building process—but I would let myself down. It would be the final straw to prove to myself that I had no idea how to be a real adult.

So I played it out. What was the worst thing that would happen if it failed? Well.

I would have to tell people Blush didn't work out.
I would have to stop seeing Blush clients.
I would have to find a different way to make a living.
I would have to keep reminding myself that I tried my hardest, and not everything works out.

Could I have handled all of that? Yes.

Did I want to? No.

But I was prepared for the worst while I continued to trudge forward. I educated myself on the boring parts of having a business and double-downed on the parts that I truly loved. And somehow, it worked. Maybe it was my effort. Maybe it was luck. Maybe it was listening to the right people. Whatever it was, I'm very grateful. But I am also well aware that Blush does not define me, and that if someday it goes away, I will be just fine.

And if you fail in one of your endeavors, you will be, too.

Become friends with "good enough."

So we've already established that the idea of perfectionism is completely and utterly subjective. People just, like, make it up.

It's fascinating, really. But it also means that if you strive for perfection in everything that you do, you will never be done. There's no real rubric to decide what is perfect and what is not. So, you'll continue to chase this impossible standard of perfection until you wear yourself out. How exhausting.

Some things in life are never meant to be complete—things like discovering new things about yourself, improving your self-esteem, or finding interesting ways to enhance friendships and relationships. Those should be never-ending processes. But homework assignments, work projects, or applications and more should have a start and an end.

This is why we need to become friends with "good enough."

If we become friends with her, then we won't feel the need to waste our energy trying to make everything perfect. We'll finish the project. We'll submit the application. We'll get to work on time. Things will be easier. And you know what? We probably won't even notice a huge difference.

They say that people who put in 20% of the effort reap 80% of the results. And guess what? The people who put in the extra 80% of the effort (giving the "perfect" 100%) only reap the remaining 20% of the results. Holy inefficient.

Let's break this down into a fitness metaphor. Because why the hell not. Let's say you want to get in shape for summer break. Pretty common. But you also have a full-time job and working out 10 hours a week while also cutting out carbs and sugar just seems like an impossible fete. But doing those things would guarantee that you meet 100% of your goal. It would also mean that you are semi-miserable because you are constantly starving and have to turn down every social engagement known to mankind because you have no time nor wiggle room in your diet.

Booooooring. So instead, you put in 20% of that effort. You cut down your calories while still eating food, and you work out thirty minutes four times a week.

I guarantee that you will see a difference. Will you be able to enter into a fitness competition? Maybe not. But was that what you were going for? No. You were aiming for a healthy body while still enjoying your life. And that's what the 80-20 rule is all about.

Become friends with "good enough." She won't let you down.

Gain perspective.

Is what you are worried about right now going to matter in five years? Be honest. Seriously. Be *really* honest. If it's a 'yes,' ok fine, let's talk. I know a lot of you have student loans that aren't going away anytime soon and I give you full permission to be pissed about it.

Or maybe you have something seriously pressing coming up that you think will definitely matter. Things like job interviews, big projects, or presentations. Maybe you gotta put in some extra effort this week. Bump it all the way up to 80%. I get it. But if not, it might be time to put the pen down and let it go.

This isn't to say that you shouldn't put effort into ANY- THING that won't matter in five years—cleaning your room is a necessary evil—but there is no need to break your back over everyday tasks. And if you don't think you will look back and remember that time when everything was perfectly tidy and there were absolutely no spelling errors (there are probably 4,756,474 in this book alone) and perfection ran ram- pant...then just let it go.

Memories aren't saved because they were perfect, memories saved because you felt something deeply. So focus on what makes you *happy*, because that's what you'll remember anyway.

Create realistic goals and expectations.

Otherwise known as, create your own definition of perfection.

Now, tread lightly here. I don't want you going off and cre- ating this absolute grandiose goal that you want to achieve by midnight. Hence, the word realistic.

We gotta hone it in. Focus on what we really want. Prioritize. And put our efforts towards the result that we know will make a difference in our lives.

The best part about this is, our goals won't look like her goals. Or his goals. Or Karen's goals. They will be YOUR goals, and these goals are unique to you. So you can't really compare them to anyone else's. And just like that, you're out of the race.

So decide what is important to you. If having a slim figure and being healthy is important to you, then that's totally fine to focus on that. But if it's not…then why would you pressure yourself to be a size 2 when it's way more natural to you to be a size 10?

The only reasonable explanation would be because society values certain sizes. But if you don't, then chances are the people you associate yourself with won't, either. So who cares? Be a fabulous size 10 and own it. These are YOUR goals. YOUR standards. YOUR perfect.

It's also very smart to have in-check expectations. Talk it out. Understand what it is that you are reaching for, and forgive yourself if the picture in your head doesn't play out in real life. To be honest, it hardly ever does. But we are resilient, and we were designed for adaptation.

Darwinism, babe.

We won't break if things don't go the exact way we planned—in fact, sometimes it works out even better. So give yourself some wiggle room in these expectations. Don't break over unmet goals, work with them. Tweak them. And keep going. Overall, if you can balance realistic goal setting, focused effort, and adaptable results, you are going to feel pretty damn good about yourself.

17

Let Go of Guilt

I know you probably feel guilty for feeling like a failure. I know you feel guilty for not reaching your potential. I know you feel guilty for not making yourself proud. I know you feel guilty for even feeling guilty at all.

So we need to get rid of it because it's bringing you down.

Here's the deal. **Guilt is meant to do one thing: incite an action.**

Apologize.
Communicate.
Act.

Otherwise, it's pretty useless. It sits and stews and eats your insides alive until you feel so completely wretched that you can't think of anything else. And what's the point of it? To punish you?

Well. Maybe. But typically we feel guilty about things that we have no business feeling guilty about. Things like not being financially sound when we are trying really hard. Or things like not being able to be in two places at once, even though we would if we could. There is no point in feeling guilty about things like that, but you still do. I know you do. Because sometimes, I do too.

So let's fix that. Part of the quarter-life crisis is harboring guilt that really shouldn't exist in the first place. And the more you let it build up inside of you, the more consumed, helpless, and lost you are going to feel. So here is a step-by-step process on how to acknowledge, confront, and let go of guilt.

Check the rationality.

Be honest. Are your thoughts rational right now? Do they logically make sense? Sometimes when we feel guilty, we tend to over-exaggerate reality in our minds. We zoom in on our actions as if they were crime scene clues, and go over every detail linking us to the remorse, anger, or embarrassment at hand. So, the first thing you have to do is check yourself.

I do this with my mom all the time. Like, all the time.

As you know, my parents got divorced when I was in college. It sucked. And I started to become overly protective of my mother. Except instead of manifesting it in a normal way, like talking about it or defending her, I constantly felt guilty.

Don't get me wrong—I loved hanging out with her. In fact, I think I used her as a bit of a crutch when I was going through a tough time. Instead of making new friends or facing the dating scene again, I would stay in and hang with my mom. It was comfortable, it was safe, and it was free. That was all I was really looking for at the time.

My mom is awesome. She's a CPA and has worked for the majority of my life. When she wasn't working she was very active in the PTA and always kept herself busy. She's opinionated and she only likes nice people. She's a whiz when it comes to finances, she champions for others' equality, and she's a dog person.

Does this sound remotely like somebody who needs to be taken care of? Not even close.

So when I started feeling guilty constantly—she quickly pointed out that I was putting this on myself and it wasn't coming from her. And she was right.

My mom didn't need me to hang out with her on Friday nights. She didn't need me to not have a relationship with my father or for me to speak poorly of him. She didn't care if I canceled our plans randomly for a fun 20-something opportunity and she didn't mind if I didn't accompany her on trips to the grocery store.

My mother is a very independent woman. She didn't need my guilt. But I kept on anyway. Why did I do this? Because I had a habit of taking on responsibility for other people's well-being and feelings.

I decided it was my job—not my mother's job—to make sure she recovered after the divorce. But that wasn't helping anybody, because not only was she fully capable of bouncing back herself, but I was making my life way harder than it needed to be. Plus, I was putting unnecessary strain on our relationship.

Anytime I started to defend myself or my actions, she felt attacked. I wasn't thinking about her feelings, I was only thinking about my guilt. And instead of acknowledging that I felt guilty, I would rationalize it and try to justify my reasoning for doing whatever I was about to do. In return, she would feel frustrated that I was getting so upset when she really didn't care. It wasn't a fun cycle.

Once I finally called myself out for my behavior, my relationship with my mother drastically improved. I actively worked on NOT feeling guilty, and was very aware when I started to crawl back into old habits. I stopped justifying my actions, and simply declined invites or told her what I was doing. And in return, she did the same.

I did not need to be taking responsibility for a grown woman's feelings. And neither should you.

So always double-check the rationale behind why you are feeling guilty. Are you taking responsibility for something that really isn't your business? Are you crossing a boundary that doesn't need to be crossed? Or did you actually do something that needs to be remedied?

If it's anything but the latter, admit that perhaps your thoughts aren't exactly rational, and let's keep going.

List the evidence.

Ok, so most likely that icky feeling you have in your gut right now isn't rational. We have already established that. So let's break it down. Why isn't this thought rational? Why is the logic simply not adding up? List it out.

Let's use something less personal (thank goodness, right?) and pretend that I feel super guilty for canceling on work because I'm sick. I have a migraine. Or a cold. Or whatever.

Anyway, I call in, explain my case, and my boss simply says "Ok, feel better." But for some reason, I feel like I should have gone in. Am I *that* sick? I don't know. Oh no. I'm lazy. I'm terrible. I should be fired. I feel...*guilty*.

So let's break it down. Here are all of the possible reasons why my guilt is not rational:

- If I have a contagious sickness (cold, flu, nausea), I could pass it along to coworkers. Going to work would actually be rude.
- My productivity would be at an all around low. Nobody works very well when they aren't feeling well.
- I could give the impression to my boss that I don't take care of myself, and might burn out easily.
- I could actually burn out and quit eventually because I didn't take time off when I needed it.
- I could frustrate my co-workers by not giving my entire 100% on joint tasks.
- I could delay my recovery process by not taking the time to chill out and recuperate, thus causing more half-ass days at work.

The list could go on and on. And what have we realized? Feeling guilty is the result of me jumping to the worst possible conclusion: *I'm lazy because I'm not taking care of myself and everybody else will notice it and care and they will HATE ME.*

Which isn't true. You are awesome and have sick days built into your employee contract. And if you don't, that means you either have a super flexible schedule where you can get your shift covered, you're in school and can get notes from somebody else, or you need a new job.

Just don't let guilt be the reason you act irrationally. Go through the evidence and make sure you are being fair to yourself.

Let go of what you cannot control.

Once you have the evidence written out (or thought out, whatever works for you), let's think about all of the things you cannot control. It's a good rule of thumb to only feel guilty for the things you CAN control. And even then, guilt does seem to be pointless.

So let's continue with the super creative example I used beforehand about calling in sick to work. Here are some things I cannot control in this scenario:

- The fact that I got sick on a weekday and not a weekend
- How other people view sick days
- How much work needed to be done on this given day
- How contagious my sickness is
- How much my condition is affecting my well-being and ability to work

Nobody asks to be sick. And the fact that I would even think about feeling guilty about it is silly. Humans get sick. That's what we do.

But I think most of us even take it a step further: **we feel like we have to be super miserable if we opt out of our responsibilities.**

We feel SO guilty that we actually believe that resting and somewhat enjoying a sick day (gasp!) is a terrible crime. Some of us might even skip out on taking medication just so we can wallow in our misery, because, hey, serves us right.

Yep. We're all crazy.

Don't let yourself feel guilty over things you cannot control, and don't let yourself feel guilty for self-soothing. As human beings, it is our right to take a break. And it is our right to not feel guilty every second of every damn day.

A-freaking-men.

Change the perspective.

If you have arrived at this step and *still* feel guilty—dang. That's impressive.

Ok, so the next thing to do is zoom out 100%, and see if you can trade places with someone else. Let's say I'm not sick, and Coach Charlotte is sick instead. She came down with a terrible migraine and really can't work today. How do I feel about this? What do I do?

- I feel really sorry for her. Migraines blow.
- I feel happy she told me so that I can be on standby to take care of any missed coaching sessions or client emergencies.
- I ask her what she is capable of doing—i.e. could you send a few notes letting your clients know that you are canceling so they can reschedule? If not I'll handle it. (This will take me about 1o minutes.)
- I let her know that I really hope she feels better and to take it easy. Poor whittle bebe.

I might be biased, but I think that's a fair estimate of how most people will view this scenario. So next time, try and put yourself in another person's shoes and see how they might feel about the situation. Hell, talk to someone else about it just to get another perspective. You'll be surprised at how hard you are on yourself, and how forgiving others are.

In fact, this trick is good in a lot of situations. Like…the quarter-life crisis.

I know you think you're failing, and I know that a lot of that stems from others' perceptions. You think that people are going to view you as harshly as you are viewing yourself.

But they're not.

The people who like you and the people who love you are fully aware that you are not struggling as badly as you think. They know that no matter how deep in the quarter-life crisis you are now—you are going to get yourself out.

So if you need a pick-me-up, ask others about their perceptions. I know it shouldn't matter what other people think—but damn, does it feel good sometimes.

Consider the action.

I know that this is just my personal belief, but I truly believe guilt is meant to spur action within us.

We feel guilty, we apologize. We feel guilty, we do the right thing. We feel guilty, we go out of our way to make it up to somebody. Guilt is the catalyst for an action.

But what if there is no action to be done? What if you are all out of actions and all you have left is just reflection and silence and misery?

Then that guilt probably isn't serving much of a purpose. It is seriously just taking up space in your mind to taunt you. And considering you are smack dab in the middle of your quarter-life crisis, don't you think you've got enough going on?

It's time to start being a friend to yourself, instead of bullying your heart from within. Guilty is a bully. Let it go.

Consider the root of the issue.

This could go a bit deep here, but have you ever asked yourself why you think you feel guilty all the time? Was guilt a major player in your childhood memories? Do the people close to you like to guilt you into doing things? Can you remember anything that might make you a bit more prone to feeling this way?

I think the reason that I felt so protective over my mother is because I don't let a lot of people into my life. I let a few special people in, and I hold on very, very tight. So when one of those people is hurting, I don't know how to handle it.

It's just too much.

My guess is that if you have a lot of people in your life, there is less impact when one of your many friends is hurt. I don't know if this is true—all I know is that it has a great impact on me when one of my chosen people hurts.

And I want to do everything I can to make sure they don't hurt. Of course, I am not in control of this, but I like to trick myself into thinking I have control by acting a certain way or spending time with someone or doing nice things. So when I can't even do the things I have convinced myself will have a diminishing effect on someone else's hurt, I feel guilty. *Extremely* guilty.

This is one of my many "roots" of why guilt as the ability to consume me. But since I know this about myself, it's easier to detect. And that makes my life a lot a bit easier. So I'd like for you to do the same for yourself. Really think about any triggers you might have that cause guilt, and see if you can break it down so you don't get caught up in it again.

Stop should-ing yourself.

Remember how I told you that you should yourself all the time?

Not shit yourself. Should yourself.

You should have a boyfriend.
You should have a better job.
You should have an amazing apartment.
You should be happy.

Stop!!! Please! Stop!!! Stop SHOULD-ING yourself!

Stop beating yourself up for these phantom accomplishments you were "supposed" to achieve. Let yourself just be!

You want to know how I already know you're awesome? Because you're worried about your future. You care. You're spiraling into a hazy fog because you are so freaked out over the fact that you might not have an awesome life. And THAT above anything else is a great indicator for the opposite. You will get through this because you want purpose. You want meaning. You want happiness. And if you want those things, you will get those things, because you will work for them. So give yourself a break.

But how? Replace "should" with "will."

I **will** *have a boyfriend.*
I **will** *have a better job.*
I **will** *have an amazing apartment.*
I **will** *be happy.*

No more deadlines, no more age limitations, and definitely no more should-ing. All this will do is build up so much guilt that you aren't where you "should" be that you are just going to burst!

Instead, turn your disappointments into GOALS. Work towards them. Understand that you ALONE have the power to chase whatever it is that will make you a fulfilled, happy human being. If you think a fancy apartment in a fancy neighborhood with a fancy Nespresso and a fancy doorman is going to make you happy—then chase the hell out of it. No judgments. Chase your bliss and don't apologize for it.

That right there is going to help mitigate your guilt by a mile. You will be guilt free of where you are in life if you can eliminate "should" and embrace the "will."

18

Negative Thoughts and Emotional Resilience

Thinking negatively can impact our life more than we even realize. We constantly have an inner monologue playing in our head. We listen to it every single day. It tells us what to say, how to act, what to do, and then processes those decisions throughout the day. So if this voice is extremely negative, that could damage our self-confidence, overall perspective, and our general mood every single day.

So how do we get rid of negative thoughts?

To be honest, the research is varied. Essentially, some psychologists, like say, Freud, believe that thoughts have underlying meaning and that everything is connected in some way. Thoughts about abandonment could stem from childhood, thoughts about sexuality probably have to do with the relationship we have with our parents, and negative thoughts are probably linked to some traumatic event in our lives.

Others believe that thoughts don't matter at all. Yep. The new trend in therapy—mindfulness—is all about disregarding thoughts and being present. Our stream of consciousness is just a bunch of random hiccups coming to the surface throughout our day. And, somewhere in the middle, is a psychologist named Beck, who coined the term Cognitive Behavioral Therapy. He decided that thoughts are important, but not always true, and that our logical brain can refute or deny the legitimacy of any thought that passes by.

So…which is it?

If I'm being honest, I'm going to say all three are probably correct when you blend them all together. I know. It's a cop out. But I think it's worth looking into each theory to try and purge negative thoughts, so I came up with the following strategy:

Decide on the level of impact.

So you're walking down the street, and BOOM, a thought crosses your mind. Is it hurtful? Silly? Random? Disturbing? How much does it affect you? Here are some examples…

"I wish I had fins."
"I am a loser."
"Being in crowds make me feel lost and scared."

It's easy to tell that these thoughts have different scales of importance. The first seems to be a pretty harmless thought. I mean, it would be cool to have fins. So let's just eliminate that one. We don't need to spend effort banning completely harmless (and sometimes interesting) thoughts.

The second one seems to be a bit more intense. Telling yourself you're a loser on a constant basis can have real damage on our self-esteem. So we can definitely pool some of our effort into throwing that one away.

The last one is pretty intense too—and there's even a trigger. Crowds = lost and scared. You gave yourself a clue! Definitely worthy of investigation.

Examine the root.

What caused this mean thought to pop up in your head? Were you perfectly happy and then BAM—a nasty gram flooded your mind? Or did something happen to trigger this mean-spirited thinking? Retrace your steps and really think about why this thought made an appearance on your typical Tuesday afternoon.

Per our examples, we've already decided to ignore the first thought. We don't need to pay too close attention to thoughts that really don't impact our days. Some thoughts are just meant to distract or entertain us, and that's it. But those other two need to be analyzed. So let's see, how did either of those two thoughts come to be?

It's probably obvious that the third thought—the one about crowds—was triggered because of an actual crowd. Maybe you were stuck in an elevator or walking through a busy neighborhood. It might not have happened simultaneously, but more likely than not you walked through a crowd sometime during that day, and the result was a thought that linked a feeling with an action. Crowds = scared. So we have that one figured out.

But what about the second thought? The thought with little to no provoking? Perhaps something super embarrassing happened or you got frustrated at work. But maybe nothing happened. Maybe this thought just popped into your head while you were driving to school or putting your makeup on the mirror. Then what?

Try your best to link some sort of action to the thought. Think about the last time you felt inferior, upset, or discouraged. Don't dwell on it—we don't want that memory to spawn more negative thoughts, but at least get a clear idea as to why this thought came to be.

Go down memory lane.

Once we have figured out a solid lead to these thoughts, it's time to dive in and see if this is a pattern in your life. The problem might not be the thoughts themselves—the problem might be a deeply embedded pattern in your life to associate negative thoughts with certain actions. And that kind of relationship must be dissolved in order to ban those nagging thoughts.

This scenario works best for the "crowd" thought. Crowds + You = Fear. You already have the trigger, but now you need to find the source and the frequency of this combination.

More times than not, just talking about the instances is going to help untangle this web. Rehashing stories, experiencing a little exposure therapy, and focusing on creating new associations with the trigger can help disband negative thoughts. However most of the time this is going to take a third party to help. Counselors and coaches are great for guiding you through the work, and an objective support system can allow you to go all in. This takes a lot of tailored work—and it's not one size fits all.

If you had a terrible experience as a child getting lost in a crowd and separated from a group, that incident could define the way you interact with crowds to this day. But, after putting in some hard work, it is possible to realign your relationship with crowds and to eliminate most of your anxiety surrounding them. Again, this doesn't happen overnight, but you can only start to tease out the problem when you have figured out where the original source is in the first place.

Build the evidence.

After you have found the root and maybe even recognized the crux of the entire pattern, it's time to debunk the premise.

For instance, when you tell yourself "I am a loser"—you aren't giving yourself ANY evidence. None. There is nothing there to the support the premise that you are indeed a loser. I guarantee you that you can find evidence in your life to support this theory—just as anyone out there can find evidence to support their own negative theories about themselves. But, the silver lining to negative thoughts, is that they tend to be automated. They aren't well thought out, and they just arrive all of a sudden. Which means you have time to gather evidence against it.

The next time you catch yourself saying something horribly awful, come up with every fact and shred of evidence possible to debunk that statement. Every piece helps.

So, if you were to tell yourself, "I am a loser," you would automatically start listing positive things in your life that contradict that statement. Things like...

I am a loyal friend.
I show up to work on time.

I pay my bills.
I read a lot.
I love others, and they love me.

This list can go on for as long as you need it to. ANYTHING that you love about yourself, that you have accomplished, that you can use as a weapon against this thought-bully is welcome. And the more you start showering yourself with reasons as to why you are not a loser, the more your thoughts will surrender to the optimism you have inundated your body with.

You can also do this with anything attached to a memory, as well. If you were concentrating on your "crowd" thought, you could simply talk yourself through all of the times you *have* been in crowds, and been fine. Build up your evidence for why you *will* be ok, and that feeling scared is actually the exception—not the rule.

Breaking down negative thoughts will also help you beef up your emotional resilience. Having emotional resilience during this time is going to act as a cushion to any of life's disappointments. You need a buffer during your quarter-life crisis to mitigate whatever shit storm is being thrown your way.

If you're not sure what emotional resilience looks like, these are a few qualities I have found to be true in every emotionally resilient person I've met.

They *don't* hang their future on bad days.

If things aren't going their way, they don't throw their hands up in the air and decide that from here on out—nothing is EVER going to go their way again. That's a little too dramatic for their taste.

Instead, they chock it up to a rut or an isolated event of crappiness. They know that things will turn around as soon as they can adjust their sour attitude. In fact, emotionally resilient people *bank* on it. They believe that over the course of their life, the net result will be positive. So whatever with these down slopes—it'll pass.

They *do* have an internal locus of control.

A locus of control is the amount of perceived control we have over our circumstances. If your locus of control is internal, that means you believe you have the power to influence your environment—for the good or the bad. If you have an external locus of control that means you believe your environment has more control over your circumstances than you do. There are positives to either one, but generally having an internal locus of control is better for our emotional health.

As a general rule, humans have a need to feel some control over their lives. We need to have reassurance that our efforts will pay off in the end. Emotionally resilient people take responsibility for their actions ("I failed a test because I didn't study hard—not because the teacher graded poorly") as well as take credit when things go their way ("they love me because I am a good person—not because they are lonely and need companionship"). These girls don't waste their energy on blaming others or finding excuses. They own up to their mistakes as well as their successes.

They *don't* beat themselves up.

The only flaw of having an internal locus of control is that it can lead to some pretty damaging effects when things go south. If emotionally resilient people believe they are in control of their destiny, then doesn't that mean that they created a situation that led them to be fired? Or dumped? Or hurt? Hmm. That sucks.

So…they have to take *all* the responsibility themselves? Well. Kinda. But most emotionally resilient people are also rational—so they at least recognize that other factors could have been at play. For example, the company was downsizing…so, although they could have been a bit more indispensable, there really wasn't anything they could do. And sure, maybe they got dumped because of their short temper, but also because there was little compatibility to begin with. As you can see, they have a little bit of the self-serving bias going on, but not enough to really affect their self-awareness.

Emotionally resilient people can see the big picture while also acknowledging what they contributed to their poor situation. They take responsibility, they forgive themselves, and they move forward. They don't sit and ruminate on any poor decisions they made or punish themselves for not trying harder. Beating themselves up does not help them get further in life. So instead they put their big girl pants on, look in the mirror, and get on with it.

They *do* have positive self-talk.

Ever sit and listen to that constant monologue playing inside your head? You know, the one that is narrating your daily happenings and walking you through your thoughts and feelings. Is it saying anything nice? Or is it a never-ending loop of profanities and insults?

Emotionally resilient people have a positive string of affirmations, encouragement, and motivation playing in their head all day long. Sure, the occasional "This sucks" or "Shoulda tried harder" pops up here and there, but overall their self-talk is genuinely positive.

They also don't concentrate on others' thoughts about them—too complicated. Way too complicated. They know that it's smarter to focus solely on their own thoughts, feelings, and actions, and try to make them as happy and positive as possible. They figure, there's enough negative language out there coming at them all day every day, might as well pick up the positive slack for themselves.

They *don't* surround themselves with negative people.

Hell to the no.

Emotionally resilient people take one look at a negative person and say "NOPE." They have worked hard to build up self-esteem, self-reliance, a positive outlook, and flexibility. Why on earth would they want to risk that by letting a negative person come in and stomp all over that?

So instead, emotionally resilient people surround themselves with people they wish to emulate. People who really bring something positive to the table. People who aren't intimidated by their accomplishments or positive disposition. Being emotionally resilient isn't just something that happens overnight—it takes work. And once people reach that level, they have to continue working at it. So risking all their hard work over a Negative Nancy simply isn't a question.

They *do* take the time to celebrate themselves and others.

Emotionally resilient people celebrate themselves and celebrate the lives of those around them. They aren't intimidated if a friend or family member happens to crush it at work. They aren't jealous when their best friends walks down the aisle before they do. And they certainly don't act like a turd in a punch bowl when a friendly coworker is promoted before them. No way. Emotionally resilient people like to enjoy life as much as possible—and if that means celebrating someone else over themselves—so be it! Celebrating is celebrating, and others deserve just as much recognition as they do.

However, they also make sure to really reward themselves for a job well done. Considering emotionally resilient people tend to take responsibility for their faults, they sure as hell throw one hell of a confidence boost party when things go their way. They know when to shower themselves with gratitude.

19

How to Stand Up for Yourself

Part of fighting off the quarter-life crisis is going to involve standing up for yourself. Life is already beating you down, and the last thing you need is anyone else taking advantage of your down-in-the-dumps mood.

I understand that you don't want to be a buzz kill. In a perfect world, you'd rather be The Go-To Girl! The Yes Woman! The Queen Bee! And Queen Bee always says yes. She takes on everything, hits it all out of the park, and comes back for more.

...in the movies.

In real life, we utilize the word "yes" way too often. It is great to do things for other people, but not at the expense of our sanity. There's a big chance the word "yes" is ruining your life.

You've got too much on your plate right now to be catering to everyone else's needs. If you are going to get out of this quarter-life crisis gratefully, then you are going to need to prioritize your time accordingly. And that involves using the word "no."

Still need convincing? Here is how saying no is going to help you move past your quarter-life crisis and into a new phase of life.

1. It creates accountability with others.

How often are you asked to do a task for someone when they could TOTALLY do it for themselves? How often do you say yes?

Bad girl.

When people habitually ask us to do favors that they are absolutely able to complete on their own, we are creating little lazy monsters. Why would they start doing anything for themselves when you're right there to do it all for them? And it's not like they're asking you to do the fun stuff. Nah. They're asking you to file the paperwork, drive two miles out of your way, or tidy up on your way out. They're asking you to do all of the things neither of you want to do. And at some point, the scale tips and it's simply not fair anymore.

It's great to do favors for others. It's wonderful to go out of your way to make someone happy. But not when it's expected. Not when it's aggressively cutting into your life. Not when it's asked out of sheer apathy.

So say no! **Embrace your inner resistance and let others become accountable for themselves.** Because when you say no, ideally they have to do something themselves. That creates productive, self-motivated, dependable people. Those are the kind of people you need to be around during this time of crisis. So if you think about it…when you say no, you are helping out everyone.

1. Higher Productivity

Another great side effect of saying 'no' is having more time to get your own shit done. When you aren't stretched incredibly thin thinking about what others need—you are able to check things off of your list and have some time to unwind. In order to be a contributing human in society, we need to be able to have time to recharge.

If we are constantly going a hundred miles a minute, we'll burn out. Or become sloppy. Or straight up quit. Dat's bad.

So by eliminating unnecessary obligations, you increase your own productivity and have more time to help others when the mood strikes you.

3. You Get to Know Yourself Better

When you're not constantly focused on doing things for others, acquiescing to odd requests, and putting your own priorities on the back burner—you clear a lot of head space. A lot. All of a sudden you get to think about what YOU want, how you would like to spend YOUR time, and what you want for YOUR future. It's crazy how different we act when our time is completely up to us. We get to use up a lot of extra time and energy towards our future goals—which may just involve helping others. But, in this case, it's because we want to—not because we feel trapped.

4. Decreases Awkward Questions

Another beautiful thing about committing to the power of "no" is the quick decrease in asks from other people. Instead, people will ask you for things when it's important or they really think you're a great fit for what they are looking for. But they stop asking you to do the things THEY should be doing for themselves. And that, in turn, decreases some awkward tension when you do in fact have to say no. We get it, it's totally awkward, but it's also totally necessary. And the more you decline, the less you are put in that situation.

Thank goodness.

5. Yes Means More

Here's the best part of saying no: it makes your YESES stand out. When you actually say 'yes' to anything—you, along with everybody else—will know that 1) you really want to and 2) you'll follow through. That right there is golden. All of a sudden you have become more reliable, honest, and trustworthy in the long run by saying no to the little things you really don't need to be doing. Your commitment and your word mean so much more. People don't question your motives or assume you're a pushover. You mean business now! So give more power to the YES by saying NO more often.

But saying 'no' is only a fraction of the behaviors you have to incorporate in order to keep your self-care intact. In fact, I was just warming you up. Learning how to set and enforce boundaries is going to be your new best friend throughout your quarter-life crisis and hopefully for the rest of your life.

But first of all, what's a boundary? *Boundaries are limits you set between you and others to keep out thoughts, activities, and other things that are not in your best interest.* Or they are also known as the line that separates where your responsibilities end and someone else's begins.

It's also worth noting that boundaries suck. They are very difficult to set, even harder to follow through with, and they never leave you feeling warm and fuzzy. But that means they're working. Boundaries are meant to keep you mentally healthy.

Without them, we lose ourselves within the context of others. We lose our ending, our beginning, our deal-breakers, our values, and our self-respect. That's a lot at stake.

So I want to make sure you are setting boundaries consis tently, appropriately, and effectively. Here is how:

First, let's do a values inventory. I'd like you to spend the next twenty minutes thinking about things in your life that you value. It could be something as general and all-encompassing as feminism, or it could be something as small as needing quiet time to recharge after working all day. Think about what you spend your money on, how you spend your time, what you value in yourself and in other people, and triggers that tend to really upset you.

You should have at least ten values written down, preferably twenty. (Ok, so this might take more than 20 minutes but I didn't want to scare you out of doing it. Sorry for lying.)

Now, you are going to be on a mission to identify scenarios and situations that violate these values. Doesn't matter if they are big or small. If you can think about a time you were deeply offended by someone else, extract the "why" and add it to your values list. This is how we know to set a boundary.

Next is the hard part. Bear with me. You must vocalize your feelings and your needs to others when they violate your values. Eeek.

So far starters, let's choose a semi-easy one. Let's say Karen is borrowing money from you on an average of once a month and never pays you back. But she always has her reasons. She lost her job, she had to pay for her cat's surgery, her car broke down, and she's due for a raise any minute now.

Karen, Karen, Karen. She really is such a sweet person, so you keep giving her money. Because you feel bad for her. And, because maybe deep down, knowing that she depends on you feels kind of nice. Eeek again.

But then you notice that she has no intention of ever paying you back. And is that a new Kate Spade bag she's carrying? And wait! I'll be damned if she's not at the local watering hole ordering a tuna tartar with a glass of cab on the side. Damn, Karen. You be shameless.

I bet you the warm and fuzzies you experience from helping a friend out have totally diminished after realizing that you've been duped.

So let's go back to your list of values and see what is being violated by Karen's actions. You might have things written down like "finances" or "appreciation" or "honesty." Technically, all of these values are being violated. How?

1. Karen taking money away from you, affecting your finances.
2. Karen not appreciating your donation in the way you had previously believed
3. Karen lying to you about how she intends to pay you back or spend the said money.

I know that normally situations in your life are not going to be this simple. A lot of times the Karen in your life isn't egregiously drowning your life's savings on Wednesday night happy hours and overpriced handbags. Maybe you just get a gut feeling that someone like Karen is violating a value, and that's good enough. We don't have to justify our boundaries. We just have to enforce them.

So, setting a boundary with Karen would look something like this:

"Hi Karen, I am not going to provide you with money anymore."

That's all. Short and sweet. Not…

"OMG Karen I totally wish I could help you out but, um, you see, I'm actually short on cash right now and you know I would TOTALLY give you WHATEVER you wanted because you are SUCH A GOOD FRIEND…but my hands are tied. I'm sorry. I'm so so sorry!" Or…

"You ungrateful BITCH Karen! You are taking my money and being reckless and irresponsible and you are going to hell in a hand basket so I hope they keep it nice and toasty for you so you burn you ass when you FALL DOWN IN FRONT OF THE DEVIL HIMSELF!"

No need to punish Karen for behavior that you have been reinforcing, encouraging, and accepting for the past however many God-forsaken months. This is just as much your fault as it is Karen's fault. You are actively allowing someone to come in and violate a value of yours, and you aren't even letting anyone know how deeply it's affecting you.

So think about the people in your life who step on your metaphorical toes. How often are you draining energy over something that you could easily stop? Are you creating greedy little monsters who come in and suck the life out of you because you refuse to stand up for yourself? Are you surrounding yourself with people who you're not even sure respect you?

Really dig deep. Because you are going to need to understand WHY you are setting a boundary, and then you are going to have to keep reminding yourself again and again.

Because here's the lovely part: **once you set a boundary, you will probably have to set it again.** In fact, I find that on average, you'll have to set it at least three times. And that might be really undershooting it.

You have more than likely already opened up a door for someone to come in and shit on all of your values. They are used to being able to do whatever they like without any consequences. So being told "no" is going to be odd for them. They are going to fight back. They are going to try again. They are going to push and push and push until they are convinced that you have left zero wiggle room in this boundary.

See? Boundaries suck.

The biggest excuse I hear on a daily basis is typically, "But I, like, hate confrontation."

Well, I would sure hope so. Who on earth LIKES confrontation? Ok, maybe lawyers. Maybe. But I still believe that some probably lie awake at night wondering if they were too harsh during their deposition. Nobody actually enjoys putting themselves in a position where someone else might walk away not liking them. The thought actually makes me cringe. We all like to be liked. We shudder at the thought of being the source of someone else's disdain.

But you know what? If you respect yourself, others will respect you, too.

It is totally worth setting boundaries with others for the sake of your well-being. Some might not like it, but those people probably shouldn't be in your life to begin with and ALSO have a high chance of falling under one of my "bad friends" categories. Consider their poor reactions and accusatory defense mechanisms as self-selection for walking out of your life.

The rest will respect your ability to "call it like it is" and stand up for yourself. Nobody likes being friends with a doormat unless they themselves are an egotistical maniac. Which again, why would you want to be friends with someone like that?

Fight for yourself. Fight for your happiness. Understand that by not setting a boundary you are reinforcing poor behavior and at some point their ability to respect you will completely disappear. Setting boundaries will not only ensure your happiness, but it will also save a relationship that has turned toxic for one or both of you. Keep your relationships and yourself healthy by communicating boundaries.

20

How to Deal with Transition

I'll state the obvious: change is hard.

I don't know what is causing your quarter-life crisis, but I know part of it has to do with either wanting to make a change or the aftermath of making the change. And regardless which side you're on—both are pee-in-your-pants frightening.

It would be lovely to think that transitions are a hop, skip and a long-ass leap to your climactic finale, but in reality, they are more like those off seasons of your favorite TV show. Think of transitions as the later seasons of *The Office* when Andy Bernard takes over as manager at Dunder Mifflin. (Yes, I still watched. Don't judge.) It's obvious the writers needed *something* to entertain us before they tied up the story lines with a bow, but what they pieced together was pretty boring and mediocre. It left us wanting to fast forward to the ending. And THAT is what a transition feels like.

It's also worth noting that most people don't talk about transition.

Instead, people recite their poignant two weeks notice letter, reenact telling off their boss off, or play the damning voicemail that finally led them to break it off with their loser boyfriend. It sounds easy, effortless, and it's extremely entertaining.

But they don't talk about the next part. The hard part. And that's because it's not glamorous. In fact, it blows. But without the tough transition, you don't get the amazing results. Sure, the catalyst will always be the story you share at cocktail parties, but we all need to be made aware of what transition is and how it makes us who we are. Because, inevitably, the quarter-life crisis is what defines us. Otherwise, we'd never change our lives.

A good rule of thumb is that **if this transition isn't painful, then you aren't making progress.**

So I want to focus briefly on how to gracefully handle transitions so you can keep chugging along with your quarter-life crisis towards that light at beginning of adulthood.

Spend wisely.

There is a major chance that you are panicking right about now. You thought your life would be SO much better once you cut ties with whatever was holding you back, but now you just feel empty. Lost. Scared. Disappointed. Insecure. Icky.

You know the old phrase "retail therapy?" No. Just, no. No no no.

It's easy to self-soothe by spending lots of money and just hoping for the best. You are in a state of limbo! You want change! You need a new wardrobe and a new apartment and a new puppy and a new LIFE! But I can guarantee you that you do not need an empty bank account. **Being frugal during this transition is only going to make your final destination feel THAT much better.**

You definitely have to spend money to make money—I know that better than everyone—but don't be irresponsible. Reckless spending is not your jam right now. A new pair of high-heeled boots might feel good in the moment, but they really won't help you get from point A to point B. That is unless you are *literally* walking there and don't mind if your toes have fallen off in the process. **Instead, invest in things that are going to challenge you to be better, not things that camouflage your fear.** Think gym memberships, textbooks, online courses, coaches (hello) therapy (hello again), organizational tools, and anything else that might make you more productive.

TL;DR: Forget the shiny glittery things and focus on what will help you reach your goal.

Stay busy.

If you sit and stew over how your life is not going how you planned—EVEN though you pulled the plug and started to actually change something—you aren't going to enjoy this transition in the least. In fact, you don't stand a chance.

Let me say this first: I am not one for distraction.

Really, I'm not. I'm a "let's face it head on and talk about it until our ears bleed and we know exactly what to do even if it really, really, really hurts" kind of person. But this falls under one of my exceptions. I'm all about the art of distraction in this scenario.

Trust me, being busy is the only thing that will make this transition fly by. If you are in school with too much time to kill, start volunteering. Get a job. Get an internship. If you are unemployed looking for a new job, spend a few hours a day searching, and then start a project. Get up and go somewhere.

Do something other than sit on your couch and wonder, "How the F did I get here?"

You probably super enjoy resting (guilty)—but you probably do not enjoy boredom. Those are two very different things. Resting is when you come home at the end of a long day, flip on the TV, and unwind. You deserve it! Hell, while we're at it, take a damn bath! Go nuts!

Boredom is when you don't have a long day at work and you just sit in the bath until it's cold because you have nothing else to do. Womp, womp.

Don't let yourself get bored. Go out and stay busy until you have a full-time purpose.

Focus on the light.

You are working towards something. But man, is it so easy to forget that when you are in the trenches. So you have to hold on to the one reason you are putting yourself through this yucky phase.

Are you visualizing what your end goal looks like? Do you picture how happy you will feel? How proud you will feel? How excited and accomplished you will feel? Do you envision that? Do you? DO YOU??

You gotta. You just gotta. Because if you aren't envisioning the light at the end of the tunnel then you are going to lose your marbles. This transition stuff is no joke and you have got to constantly remind yourself that it's not for nothing.

Bonus: Focusing on your final destination will also keep you on track.

It's easy to get lost in the mess of the direction of your life. And it's even more overwhelming if you aren't crystal clear on where it is you want to land. You can have some flexibility, yes. That's totally acceptable. But not focusing on the job, the city, the feeling—that is a big mistake. You should be architecting the blueprint of your life during your free time. That way you can focus on the light and not on the shade of gray you are living in right now.

Talk it out.

A lot of people feel really ashamed about feeling stuck. The irony is, the majority of all 20-somethings have felt super stuck at one point or another, and all they wanted to do is talk about it, too! But oh...it's so embarrassing. No one wants to admit life isn't turning out the way they wanted. Especially not when Facebook is a glowing advertisement for how EVERY-ONE ELSE IS DOING BETTER.

So be the brave one. You have to get this out of your system. Harboring feelings of shame, uncertainty, fear, anxiety, sadness, anger, and frustration is never a good idea. Swallowing your feelings whole will not make this next year(s) any easier. Instead, you'll probably develop acid reflux and, on occasion, forget how to breathe.

You are not pathetic for feeling like you made a giant mistake or that your plan didn't work out.

Of course, you are going to have doubts! You just made a rather risky decision to change your life. Most people don't do that. Most would rather soak up the consequences of not changing rather than putting themselves out there. And trust me, putting yourself out there is NOT fun and it is NOT sexy. It is terrifying. But that's what you are doing right now. **You are**

TRYING to create something better for yourself, and that is excruciatingly vulnerable. You deserve a cookie. Or 12.

I get that talking about it leads to people knowing your secrets. But not everyone is Gretchen Wieners and a lot of people simply want to be there for you. It's ok to take off your armor and be real with others. Pride holds most of us back (it is definitely my biggest vice), but your feelings are more important than others' perception.

So talk about it. Talk about how you aren't taking the easy way out. Let someone know about the doubt and anxiety and fear that you are feeling. Process it out loud. The more you hold it in the more you are going to let your doubt consume you, and eventually, it will take the helm and steer you back to boring, tedious safety.

You don't want that. You made this change for a reason. So talk about it OUT LOUD with someone who is going to help you comb out reality from fear. Obviously, I have a good idea as to where you can find this help, but I'll leave that up to you. Talking about icky things is the brave thing to do. So why stop short? Keep being brave and this is going to pay off.

21

The 10 Commandments of the Modern Girl

You are going to have a lot of self-doubt over the next few months. It comes with the territory. So instead of succumbing to any of your insecurities, I'd like for you to have a quick read you can turn back to in order to remind yourself that you are incredible. The 10 Commandments of the Modern Girl are not to be taken lightly—they are to be taken in slowly and practiced consistently.

1. Thou Shalt Not be Defined by a Relationship Status

A relationship status is not the end all be all for the modern girl. She is allowed to enjoy being single, being in relationships, being engaged, being married or even enjoy being divorced. She's also not determined to rush to the next step, either. Marriage is a possibility, not the inevitability. Lastly, modern girls are also not limited to friendships that mirror their own phase in life. She has friends in many different relationship statuses, and it only enhances the bond.

2. Thou Shalt Say No

The modern girl no longer has time for anything and everything people ask of her. The myth of "having it all" has somehow also convinced us that we have to say "yes" to every chore, every appointment, and every position that comes our way. But the reality is, "having it all" is about prioritizing. She gets to choose what she wants in her life, how she balances it, and what she values the most. And in order to do that, she has to say no to certain things.

3. Thou Shalt Not Harbor Guilt

As much as the modern girl may really like her ability to care for others and to show empathy, she doesn't also have to feel really, really, bad when negative things occur outside of her control. She doesn't have time for guilt. She knows that it is an ugly emotion; one that stays far beyond it's welcome and distracts her from her priorities. She doesn't need to feel guilty for getting a position someone else wanted, or for prioritizing her time over other things. So, she won't. She releases it, and moves on.

4. Thou Shalt Not Habitually Apologize

Modern girls apologize when it's necessary, not when it's routine. If someone bumps into her on the street, she won't apologize for it. If someone interrupts her while she is speaking, she won't apologize for it. And if someone hurts HER feelings, she won't apologize for it. Apologies are necessary when SHE has done something to hurt another person. Otherwise, you probably won't get anything from her, because it's not her job. She will continue on as she was, and that is what should be expected.

5. Thou Shalt Sit at the Table

Sheryl Sandberg has officially asked every modern girl to 'Sit at the Table', a phrase meant to encourage us to put ourselves out there in the workforce. But, this is more than just deciding to sit at the round table discussion instead of grabbing the free chair in the corner–it's about the modern girl speaking up for herself. Asking for the raise. Going for the promotion. Speaking her mind. Contributing her ideas. It's time for the modern girls to see themselves as worthy, intelligent, and capable as men, even if it means putting extra energy to be recognized. The modern girl won't accept NOT being at the table–because that's where she belongs.

6. Thou Shalt Not Compare

As Theodore Roosevelt so gracefully put it, "comparison is the thief of joy." The modern girl is not imprisoned by constant comparison of her figure to other bodies, her intelligence to other brains, or her accomplishments to others' careers. She is her own entity, and she only compares herself, to herself. Other stories of ambition and success only drive her to do better. She is on her own path, and it cannot and will not be compared with another's.

7. Thou Shalt Let Go of Toxic Relationships

The modern girl is not afraid to be the CEO of her life. She promotes, demotes, fires, and hires people as she wishes. She has high standards for her friendships and relationships and doesn't let other people drag her down. She can still be forgiving and caring, but she doesn't let others walk all over her. If someone in her life takes advantage or exhausts her energy, then it's not lost on her that it might be time for them to leave. She wants to maintain a positive, optimistic, and ambitious attitude, and sometimes it's borderline impossible with close friends who refuse that lifestyle. But, on the flip side, she values and loves her friends who bring out the best in her, and she tries to bring out the best in them.

8. Thou Shalt Embrace Imperfections

The modern girl doesn't have the perfect body because nobody has the perfect body. So, she chooses to embrace her imperfections such as her odd-looking toes, lack of a thigh gap, cute double chin, or frizzy hair. They make her who she is, and hell, she likes who she is. So why not like all of it? Magazines can continue to be Photoshopped and friends can continue to wear smaller jean sizes, but that doesn't affect her vision of herself. She knows she's a gem, and that's all that matters.

9. Thou Shalt Support Each Other

The modern girl is not threatened by other's successes. In fact, they inspire her. Successes for women in general are positive for the modern girl because that only creates more opportunity for her. She knows that for her to succeed, women need to succeed. She embraces achievements and awards given to other women EVEN if she does feel a twinge of jealousy because she knows that it only helps her and her gender in the long run. So she puts her energy into supporting others, and she feels pretty fabulous about it.

10. If Thou Shalt Choose a Partner, Thou Shalt Choose a Real One

If the modern girl does choose a partner, she makes sure that person is an actual partner. She is a strong proponent of equal duties and responsibilities. She will pick a partner who will support her, push her, love her, and challenge her. She looks for someone who will help inside the house and outside of the house. Someone who will make compromises to support their relationship as a whole and their individual successes. Someone who doesn't tolerate an imbalance of power in their relationship. Not because she demands it, but because they wouldn't have it any other way.

Conclusion

You did it. You read this entire book and survived. And if you can do that, then you can survive this quarter-life crisis.

I know you feel like you've lost your glow, but it's still there. I promise. You are a warrior who is now armed with tools and perspectives that will help you fight off the enemy of confusion and hopelessness. And with each day that you continue to fight, your glittery optimism will slowly crawl back in.

Never stop believing that you are special. I don't care what asshole Millennial-hater wants to beat down your spirit out of their own insecurity—don't believe them. You are special and you will continue to be special—even in this slump. Why? Because you are determined. You don't give up. And you have spent more years believing in yourself than you have doubting yourself. This is not the pattern of your life—it is the outlier.

I know you don't want to hear this right now, but you are going to be such a better human for this crisis. You are going to have a greater appreciation for success, for friendship, for love, and for kindness. You are always going to remember how terrible this felt, and you will always have a greater sense of empathy for somebody else's struggle. Feeling hopelessness and feeling rejected are two of the worst feelings to experience on this planet, and you have probably felt both. So take that experience and use it for the betterment of your own life.

If you need anything along the way, you know where to find me.

Blush you.

About the Author

Kali Rogers is the CEO and Founder of Blush Online Life Coaching. She earned her BA in Psychology from The University of Texas in Austin and her MS in Counseling from Southern Methodist University in Dallas. She currently resides in Los Angeles, California where she spends the majority of her time working with her fabulous clients, running her company, Blush, and facilitating corporate training across the country. Her passion is helping females, especially 20-somethings, tap into their authentic selves in order to achieve their goals and reach peak happiness. She loves closing the gap between where her clients currently are and where they never dreamed they'd be. In her spare time, she also manages effortlessly burn things in the kitchen, hunt down restaurants that serve Texas-style queso, devour *Parks and Rec* reruns, text with Caroline, and of course, snuggle with her fiancé while he makes her watch "critically acclaimed" (but also sometimes boring) movies.

Twitter
@thisiskali / @joinblush
Instagram
@thisiskali / @joinblush
Facebook
facebook.com/kalielizabethrogers / facebook.com/joinblush
Website
http://joinblush.com